MAXIMIZE YOUR POTENTIAL

Experience How God's Power Works Within You to Realize an Abundance of Prosperity in Every Area of Your Life

Bishop Jerry L. Maynard

Word of Life Ministries

Maximize Your Potential
by Bishop Jerry L. Maynard

Printed in the United States of America
ISBN 0-9712106-0-2

Unless otherwise indicated, Bible quotations are taken from the King James Version.

Cover Designer
Peggy Lyle Jennings
Pat Everage

Distributor
J.L. Maynard Ministries
4300 Clarksvillie Pike
Nashvillie, TN 37218

Publisher
Word of Life Ministries
300 Clarksvillie Pike
Nashvillie, TN 37218
(615) 876-8749 ext. 254

Donna

May you life become the
example that God has
ordained it to be.

Shalom,

Jerry L. Pinyard

Preface

In 1981, while experiencing difficult times in my life, I questioned God about all that I had experienced and the many things I had lost. My preoccupation with the things I lost was hindering me from moving forward with my life and from gaining new experiences.

It was while on my knees praying, that the Lord introduced me to a faith moving realization. What He said to me was to forget about the things that I had lost and to thank Him for the things I had left, regardless of how things appeared.

It was also during this time of prayer that He reminded me of His word found in Ephesians 3:20, "Now unto him that is able to do exceeding abundantly above all that we ask or think, according to the power that worketh in us." At that time, unlike any other time that I had read that scripture, the words seemed to leap from the page and deposit themselves into my spirit. This revelation has become the moving force in my life, to maximize my potential.

I have actually lived the life of taking a little and making more. Because of my experiences of how God's power worked in me to realize abundance in every area of my life, I pondered how this message could help others who are going through similar situations. The thought of writing this book became very pronounced.

In the following chapters it is my intention to show how one can move from a posture of purposelessness to purpose, from abandonment to belonging, from hopelessness and helplessness to a posture of fulfillment.

This book lets you know that your greatest hour has not passed, rather, it is yet to come; and you determine the major factor of its magnitude. Whether you have just begun your Christian walk or are one who has sown good seed and are standing on the promises of our Lord and Savior, know that the time of harvest is here! Prepare yourself now, and learn how to be receivers of the abundance of God. *"Maximize Your Potential."*

Foreword

Salvation is a gift that is available to all mankind through Christ Jesus, Who lived, was killed and arose so that we may be saved from a life of sin. While salvation is the greatest gift of all, it is not the "end all" of our Christian walk. God, through His Word, makes precious promises of an abundant life for believers. That life can only be realized by living the life and purpose that He has set forth for each of us. With that life of purpose, He gives to us the means by which we can achieve it. Potential.

Maximize Your Potential is an exceptional collection of thought provoking, call to action instruction that impels us to put into practice Christ's teachings. Manifestations of deliverance, divine revelation and transformation await you in every page and paragraph.

Bishop Maynard converses with us on a personal level, how to discover God's purpose for our lives by always employing Him first. He helps us to see ourselves the way God sees us, confident and able to accomplish the impossible. He sets out for us the need for spiritual transformation so that we can either be ready for battle, or, know when the battle is not ours, but the Lord's. He shows us how the Spirit of God works in us providing everything we need, and that when we trust in Him to meet our need, we start to learn who we are and how great He is.

Because of his works, his commitment to God and the people of God, it is a privilege to introduce to you this work by my friend, Bishop Jerry L. Maynard. Bishop Maynard has worked with me for many years in numerous capacities representing the Church of God in Christ, and in organizing the annual *Soul Winners* Conference. I consider him an outstanding churchman, administrator and educator, a man of great integrity and discipline.

Bishop Maynard speaks from the Word of God, so there's nothing new in what is said. But, we need to hear it over and over. And Bishop Maynard "*puts it in the context of where we are today.*" This is a special honor for me.

Bishop Gilbert E. Patterson
Presiding Bishop, Church of God in Christ

Introduction

The Christian ultimate dilemma is how to incorporate the sustaining power of a relationship with Christ into daily living in the secular world. In my experience, both of these forces are brought together when you maximize your potential for Christ in the world. What this means is that you utilize the gifts that Christ has given you to accomplish and live out your vision of a productive life. And, your success in the world becomes a testimony to others about Christ since He is the source of that experience.

I believe that until there is a critical examination of the inner self, there can be no opportunity to maximize that potential in the tangible areas of life such as family, career, and finances. Our emphasis on these significant areas, although they are not the sum total of human experience, stems from persuasive evidence that they are extremely difficult for individuals.

My hope for you is that you realize that Christ has already equipped you with the tools necessary to maximize your potential, both in the spirit and in society. Next, I hope you discover what God has ordained for your life so that you can put into practice what you have read. But, most importantly, I hope that you come to understand that your worldly success is simply a microcosm of your greater relationship with Christ.

Contents

Chapter One

Discovering Your Purpose

"Our spiritual awakening does more to inform us of our purpose than the intellectual blueprint designed by the rational mind."

One of the most revealing traits of man is his need to dominate the environment around him. He exhibits this quality through the strategic manner in which he advances in life, thus providing evidence that man can accomplish his will if only he exerts himself. While elements of man's argument for wanting to control his own life are valid, it is the blatant absence of man's recognition of God's authority that dooms him to failure.

There must be a revision of how we view God's place in our lives. While there may have been a period when God was reverently relegated to noon on Sundays, we must now consider an active repositioning of His role. How does His sovereignty figure in the decisions of your life? Where is God in terms of your priorities? On a spiritual level, there must be an examination of our submission to His will. If that is not in place, it becomes difficult for us to recognize and enjoy His efforts and blessings in our lives. What is the point of asking God for help if we deny having heard His words when they are in conflict with our flesh? We must mature to a spiritual level where we can concede that our blessings appear in proportion to our degree of submission to His will.

This revision will affect our lives in practical as well as spiritual ways. And, for many Christians, it is the practical changes that can be the most challenging. The reason for this is that we sometimes value those whom we see more than we value the One who sees all. It is one thing to be a believer on Sunday, when the environment of a church service is conducive to praising God. But, the true test of faith is whether we can praise Him through the difficulties of our spiritual journey.

It is naïve to suppose that a deepening of our relationship with Christ will not affect our homes, jobs and relationships. If you make Christ the head of your household, would that not challenge society's paradigm of your family's hierarchy? If your manner in the workplace began to reflect Christ, would that not elicit a surprising range of responses from co-workers? Imagine if you allowed God to direct you in your relationships; would you not experience real love for others that would reflect Christ's love for you? Can you imagine the dramatic changes in your life if you loved Christ with an intensity that was the same as or greater than your love for the people and things of the world? If there is no transformation in your life after you have deepened your bond with Christ, you may want to examine if any "deepening" has actually occurred.

If you are in submission to God's will, expect people in your life to be affected. This distancing or renewal of relationships will occur with family, friends, mates, co-workers and your church family.

Have you ever wondered why someone who was always close to you is no longer there? Why the man or woman you loved more than life itself has slipped from your embrace? Think about whether they were so important to you that pleasing them took precedence over pleasing Christ. God has to remove certain people from your life so that you are released from their worldly influences. He needs to isolate you so that you will see and hear Him. One can imagine how Christ must grieve to see how much we give of ourselves to people who do nothing for us, and how little we love Him who does everything for us.

The Word is apt when it states, "The Lord giveth, and the Lord taketh away." While God segregates us from certain people, He also offers the balm of new Christian associates. These persons may be placed in your life as a support system during your Christian growth. Others He may give you so that you can be a testimony to the power of a personal relationship with Christ. In this way, you become a model for others in their Christian journey.

Your recognition of God as the sovereign force and Creator in your life is required before He can prepare you to discover the true purpose of your life. God reveals to us in His Word who we are in Christ. And, that self-knowledge is the key to understanding that you have a distinct role in God's plan. He wants to use your life not only to glorify Him, but also to serve as a testimony to others. Revelation 12:11 says, "And they overcame him by the blood of the Lamb, and by the word of their testimony; and they loved not their lives unto the death." Imagine that your life, with all its deficiencies, can be empowered to bring other people to Christ! It is an exciting idea, but one that carries great responsibility. And, the discovery of our purpose is a facet of Christian growth that presupposes greater developments in our relationship with Christ.

The greatest misconception you must get rid of is that you are the main force in your life. Your efforts alone have not brought you to the place you now occupy in life. The Word of God declares, "For in Him we live, and move, and have our being" (Acts 17:28a). This concept may appear perverse, or at least ridiculous. Competitive and self-seeking efforts are continuously fostered and applauded in society. Individuals are taught that they are the greatest factor in creating their success. According to that rationale, it would appear clear that your material accumulation is a direct result of your hard work, your job title a tribute to your talent, your car a reflection of your personal ambition, and your home a sign of your having arrived.

Yet, the irony of America's deceptive adages regarding the individual's ability to achieve is that they negate the possibility that there is a power operating in our lives other than self. From infancy, people are taught that they are in control of their lives. One need only observe how a baby finds joy, not only in the discovery of his hands, but more often in the ability to manipulate those hands himself. So, from infancy on, we begin a process that encourages a lifetime preoccupation with control. It is only the degree of finesse with which we move the forces in our lives that either garners man's respect or contempt. So, by adulthood, we have fairly well established the self as the source of power and strength.

This perception of self alienates us from the true source of power: God. And, that separation keeps us from discovering who we are in Christ and what He has for us. If a computer is not connected to a source of power that can mobilize its capabilities, it will not be able to function properly. In like manner, we need to recognize that we cannot propel our life to the level God has planned for us without being connected to Him.

It is critical to understand that you are here for the powerful purpose of maximizing your potential. In order to do so, you must know what potential you have. Knowing your purpose provides you with this information. An aspect of that awareness is the understanding that God has allowed you to be here today. The value of reflecting upon the reason for our continued existence is that it leads to one compelling answer.

We are here to glorify God by allowing ourselves to be used as His instrument. And, we can only be effective as an instrument when we utilize all of what God has given us.

He has called each of us, irrespective of our specific purpose, to greater service and greater responsibility. According to I Corinthians 7:7, "But every man hath his proper gift of God, one after this manner, and another after that." Essentially, we must allow our lives to be an example before the unsaved. In this way, we become God's instrument in bringing others to Him. If your life is blessed and the unsaved see great rewards as a result of your faithfulness, will that not encourage them to at least learn who Jesus is? Since we are committed to operating as a vessel for His glory, we can more fully serve the Lord. It is an act of service not only on your part, but on behalf of people you illuminate about Christ.

Your ability is as great as your willingness to allow God to use it for His good. It is important that you understand that your purpose is interconnected with your capacity to serve Him. This is because, if you focus on self, you will find there is not enough to sustain you in life. But, if you say, "Lord, here I am and all that I have. Use me and let Your will be done," then you are allowing Him to transcend your limited abilities.

An important question to consider is why God specifically chose you to do His will. While responding to His call on your life is an awesome responsibility, it is also an incredible opportunity for blessings. Have you ever considered why you are here? Not here simply in the physical sense, but also in terms of the mind, spirit and personality. When many people drew their last breath yesterday, why were you allowed the opportunity to see a new day? Consider how you avoided danger and death today. Why did God smile upon you? What is it about you that caused God to look upon you and say, "Live"? Life is not a gift to be taken for granted, but a symbol of possibility and change if you are sensitive to what God is directing you to do with it.

You may believe that in your Christian walk you have illustrated some incredibly elusive quality that convinced God you deserved to be here a little longer than your hell-raising neighbors. Surely there is evidence to support your claim of being a model born-again, lake-baptized, choir-leading, tongue-speaking, tithe-giving, Holy Ghost-shouting believer. These things should count for something with a Lord who knows you never missed a Sunday!

Yet, this calls for us to put off our cloak of Christian righteousness and recognize that no one but Christ can see us for whom we really are at this time. This is the period when you must look into His mirror without a mask. In recognizing that in this moment you are facing Him alone, can you truthfully say you have done anything to be DESERVING of God's commitment, presence, and dedication?

We can never deserve these gifts from God. We are fallible, and because of our human nature we are incapable of achieving this. "For all have sinned, and come short of the glory of God" (Romans 3:23). Yet, He blesses us anyway. It is incredible that, although we fail, God continues to extend these life supports to us. Have we done anything that causes God to look at us and say, "I want to use you as an instrument?" When we exhibit a willingness to be used, God responds by placing us in an opportune situation to be a part of His kingdom building. And, if we do not respond to that opportunity, He uses another vessel because His will is always done. Evidence of His power is how He can take the very people we would never have chosen to teach us about His commitment and love for us.

So, through reflection and communing with God, we can come to understand His reason for allowing our continued existence: it is so that we can discover our purpose. "Purpose" does not simply refer to the type of job we are going to have, although it refers to discovering how God plans to use us to glorify Him. If we understand that our ONLY reason for being placed here is to glorify God, it becomes less challenging to put aside our personal agendas. Following your personal dreams is fine, but not to the exclusion of listening to what God has for your life.

It is as simple and as difficult as reprioritizing our life to better serve God and others. The simplicity of choosing to serve God is made possible by knowing that our lives are blessed and that we can enter into His gates. It makes sense to place Him over every aspect of our lives. We know in our hearts that He is responsible for us, and acknowledging His Lordship will create the best quality of life for us.

But, the challenge comes when we resist the guidance of Christ and the shallowness of our faith is exposed. It is not easy to submit to God against society's paradigm of control and power. Society does not recognize Christ; it recognizes individuals' ability to subdue their environment and invoke change. So, the complexity of a life with Christ resides in the ability to trust, not in the visible world, but in the Spirit. We are reminded of this in 2 Corinthians 4:18, "While we look not at the things which are seen, but at the things which are not seen: for the things which are seen are temporal; but the things which are not seen are eternal."

Once we have heard God's call to our unique purpose, we must accept responsibility by fulfilling that purpose. It is our obedience in this area that garners His commitment, presence, and recognition. The commitment of God is that He will never forsake us or leave us in time of trouble.

Humans, even spouses who have taken the legal and spiritual vow to commit to us, will fail, because people are not perfect and the wavering of their commitment to us on any level is a painful and alienating event.

But, the beauty of God's love is that He is always there. Have you ever met a parent, lover, or friend who could make the same claim? Has anyone always stood at your side? Have they loved you when you were not at your best? Have they stood by you when you disappointed and hurt them? Only God is capable of that kind of commitment. That is the beauty of His love. So, when He asks you to live out your purpose for His sake, you must believe that He is with you through all your efforts. Matthew 28:20b reminds us of His presence with us: "...and, lo, I am with you alway, even unto the end of the world. Amen." Not only does He commit Himself to us, but also He allows us to reside in His holy presence as Christians. Our acceptance of and belief in Christ assures us a place with God. If we are in Him, then He is in us as well (John 15:4). And, the fact of God's presence guarantees His rich blessings. While these may include material prosperity, the greatest wealth is in our shared relationship with Christ and the fulfillment of living according to His spiritual design.

Another benefit of accepting God's purpose for us is that He blesses those Christians living in compliance with His word. How can good things not happen to you when God is ordering your steps? The problem with the methodical blueprint we create for our lives is that our intellectualism will not protect us from human fallacy. Our planning is only successful to the extent that we enlist the Lord's assistance. When that is done, God blesses us both privately and, oftentimes, publicly for our obedience.

When we are living in His will, we please Him and He blesses us. So, we must first learn what our purpose is, accept the responsibility that comes with it, and fulfill it. We can fulfill our purpose through various employments and efforts; we must remember, however, that the purpose of having a purpose is to exalt His name and good works.

Each person must discover his or her own role in society as dictated by God. And, it is empowering to know that you have been called for kingdom building. Such was the case for the Apostle Paul in the Bible.

When Jesus met Paul on the way to Damascus, He called him to His purpose. When the greatness of Jesusĺ light caused Paul to fall from the beast he was riding, other things in his life "fell away" as well. When Paul lost himself in the presence of the Sonof God, he lost sensibility along with his equilibrium. More importantly, he lost what he considered to be his purpose: the need to persecute Christians.

The destiny he had carved out for himself was changed as a result of God calling him to a mission he never would have chosen. This is important because not every call is necessarily the path we would choose. Yet, there is the promise that God is calling us to a higher place in life then we could visualize on our own. He promises greater rewards than we could ever imagine. All Paul knew was that there was a great light that he could not handle. Paul's experience is recognizable to any Christian who has ever believed that he/she is doing the right thing without receiving direction from God.

Here was a man who had studied at the feet of Gamaliel, who was learned and disciplined as well as imbued with the Greek culture. He was a citizen of the Rome and a Jew of the tribe of Benjamin, which was highly favored. Paul was recognized as being astute, wealthy, and intellectual. He certainly seemed to be a man of the "inner circle," even today. Yet, he was a man not yet living in accordance with His purpose. You must understand that discovering your purpose is usually a process of becoming increasingly aware of what you are to do for God. Or it can be a single life-changing event, as it was for Paul.

Paul did not initially understand that the Christians he was trying to incarcerate, and kill had been given the task of evangelizing the world for Jesus. Paul was attempting to keep Christians from fulfilling their purpose of moving in accordance with God's direction. How many times have Christians' well-meaning remarks discouraged the spirit of someone from believing in their call? How many times have we made such remarks or been the person who was discouraged? But, the power of God is such that He can move His enemies to do His will and thus ensure that His kingdom on earth is being realized.

God understands that many of us need to identify with others in kingdom building. And, we can more easily identify with people than with the spirit. Thus, God wisely chooses people through whom He changes our lives. When Jesus met Paul,

He instructed him to go to Damascus and find a street named Strait. There he would find Ananias and receive an anointing. Like Paul, many of us need an anointing in our lives. We need to be filled with the Holy Ghost and changed. If you have tried living your way, haven't you had enough experience to convince you that you cannot do it alone? Allow the Holy Ghost to fill you with the expectancy of deeper and richer living.

The purpose of Ananias laying his hands on Paul was not so much for Paul to feel his touch as to receive the anointing of God. As a result, He could use Paul as His instrument. It was never Ananias' hands but the anointing of God conveyed through his hands that caused Paul's shackles to come off, leaving him liberated in Christ. It was the anointing that healed Paul's blindness so he could see both physically and spiritually. And, this anointing and Paul's acceptance of God's purpose are what transformed Paul into the greatest evangelist in Christian history.

Paul understood a critical point about discovering your purpose in God: it is a personal matter in which you must step out on the authority God has given you. Paul was not chosen by anybody but Jesus to be a disciple. In the salutation of his letters, he refers to himself as "Paul, the prisoner" or "Paul, the disciple of Jesus Christ." He refers to himself in this way because mankind did not choose him for his purpose. The book of Ephesians begins with "Paul, an apostle of Jesus Christ by the will of God." Paul has been called by the will of God. Why is this important, and how does it relate to us today?

Paul is saying that he knows he has been called for a specific purpose but also understands that not everyone recognizes its validity. The Apostle Peter would not recognize his call because he (Paul) was not one of the original Twelve. But, Paul's response was essentially, "If God loves me and accepts me, as deficient as I am, then who are you to tell me whether or not I can serve?" How often do we question or even deny the validity of someone's call to do something, without recognizing that we may be keeping him from his purpose? Yet, regardless of others' response, Paul knew he was called to preach to the Gentiles even when other disciples refused to.

Like Paul, those who do not believe that we were called for a certain purpose will confront us. But, we must see that confrontationas an opportunity to strengthen our faith. Regardless, we must fulfill the role for which God has made us responsible. We need to be where the spirit of God is expressed, the love of God is realized, the truth of God is preached, and the mercy of God is extended.

Paul also understood that he was responsible for fulfilling his purpose despite any obstacles. He understood that even if he was never invited to preach in the synagogue or the temple or allowed to evangelize in the inner circles, God would still hold him accountable for fulfilling his call. There were certain barriers that Paul had to overcome, and we should expect to have to do the same as we move into the will of God. Paul experienced alienation from other disciples, was rebuked by the Jews to whom he witnessed, and had the singular experience of being directed to preach to the Gentiles.

Sometimes, rejection from the world is necessary to provide us with the empathy and knowledge we will need. If Paul had not experienced alienation and rejection, he would not have appreciated the dilemma in which the Gentiles found themselves. In the same way, we must be prepared for difficult situations even when we are living in accordance with God's will. While they may not appear so at the time, these situations are tools of preparation that allow us to better fulfill our calling. Romans 8:28 states, "And we know that all things work together for good to them that love God, to them who are the called according to His purpose." Did it ever occur to you that the experience you are going through is less about you than about preparing you to later testify to someone else in similar conditions?

Paul knew his purpose was to teach the unteachable, to reach the unreachable, and to preach to the downcast of society who battled seducing spirits, witchcraft, and pagan idols. On the surface, it would not appear to any of us that Paul was placed in a particularly valuable situation. How motivating is it to exist among the poor and outcast when other people are placed in positions of esteem and prosperity? Likewise, how often have we been disobedient to God because the place where He was calling us to go was not what we had envisioned? We say "Lord, you placed that person in that position, and yet you allow me to toil for You in obscurity and poverty." We have to learn that we are never placed in a position where we are not being developed for greater works. Further, when we question God's plan for us, based on what we see Him doing for someone else, we are exposing our lack of faith in Him.

So, while preaching to the Gentiles did not result in esteem for Paul, its value lay essentially in the benefits for the Gentiles who were receiving the Word. If we are honest, we must acknowledge that we have all experienced some of the difficulties that the Gentiles faced. Other people may not realize this, but there has been a time when you were rejected and alienated from the group you held up as the standard. There was a time when people did not accept you and when you made unwise decisions that distanced you from God. It does not matter what you did or who you were in the past; if you asked God to forgive you and help you, then it was done. And, if He saved you and placed His Word in you, then you are seen as if you had never done anything wrong.

It is not the longevity of your experience with God that matters, but whether you are committed to Him right now. If you have been in the church 40 years, but 29 of those years you raised hell, what good have you been? It is what you are doing now that matters. You have to get to a point where you say to God, "I understand why I am here. I understand what my purpose is." Just as God sent

Paul to the Gentiles so they could hear the Word, there is a word for you today.

When Paul wrote to the church at Ephesus, one of the churches that he loved so much, he touched on how the Gentiles felt they would never measure up to the Jewish people. The Gentiles felt this way because of all the terrible things they had experienced. They were comparing themselves with the Jews and felt that they were not good enough. This very act of comparison sets one of the parties up for failure.

The same comparisons are made in society. There are those in society that would judge us based on how much we have. If your job does not generate the same income as theirs, they will make you feel as though you do not belong. You may be happy being a dishwasher, but because someone else stigmatizes you because of your position, it changes your perception of yourself. You sometimes lose your happiness because you do not feel you are measuring up to others. These kinds of activities within our society have caused many problems within the psyche of man.

Society relies on externals to ascertain a person's value. These externals relegate many worthwhile individuals to the margins of society, individuals who do not measure up by these standards. How can one's level of education alone be the deciding factor in determining one's wisdom and practical knowledge? There are a lot of educated fools. If we followed society, we would not assign value to countless saints because they did not have access to certain opportunities.

While the world deliberates over your human vitality and allots points based on socioeconomic status, employment, and highest degree earned, you must move with the assurance of Christ's acceptance. He is most concerned with your internal willingness to be used as an instrument of change. Remember that at David's anointing, God looked into his heart (1 Samuel 16:7). Further, Christ cares about the depth of our experience with Him, not the superficial trappings that serve to create more barriers.

Man is trying his best to reach levels beyond what he has already explored. He wants to achieve greater heights that seem to represent progress. But, we must understand that not all persons may be able to occupy the same place in society. Each of us must discover who we are and what His purpose is for us. And, once we learn these things, we can understand why things happen the way they happen, and why we are where we are at this particular time. Then, we can learn what to do in the position in which we have found ourselves.

This same insecure and critical spirit of comparison can be found in the church. Think about those persons who are always praying and always singing the praise hymns. You think these things are a reflection of how deep their relationship with God is. You have the impression that they are praying and praising because they are so happy in the Lord.

For many of these people, this is the only way they could make it. If they did not pray and sing at the top of their lungs, they simply would not be able to handle the problems of life. You believe they are doing it because of the depth of their relationship with Christ, when in fact their behavior is often the truest evidence of the shallowness of their relationship with Him.

It is often these misconceptions that have new Christians doubting their relationship with Christ. You have to become comfortable with who you are in Him without using other Christians' response as your standard. So, do not compare yourself to anyone else. Pick up the Word of God and find out who you are and where you ought to be. Paul was essentially telling the church at Ephesus that he wanted them to know who he was, and that he was then going to share who they were in God.

God has blessed us with every spiritual blessing in heaven (2 Peter 1:3). Whatever is in heaven, whatever the citizens of heaven, realize the Lord has blessed us with these things. This is what Paul was sharing with the Gentiles. He is saying to them, "I realize that you are Gentiles and that you have not measured up to the expectations and standards of the Jewish people, but the Lord has already blessed you and you do not have to wait for any further blessing." God loves and accepts into His kingdom those whom man rejects; therefore He is a far greater ally than mere man.

Paul's message is just as applicable to us today; we need only exchange the word "Gentile" for our name. God is essentially saying, "Jerry, you don't have to go through an obstacle course to get where I want you to be; I've already blessed you right where you are." God is saying that you are special to Him right now. Others may not want you to feel this way, but you are blessed.

God chose us in Christ before the world began. While you may not understand why you are where you are today, God knows. He planned for you to be here today. While you are going through the process of understanding what your purpose is, it may be helpful to know he ordained that purpose before you were born (Jeremiah 1:5). If God, the Creator of all things, ordained your purpose before you drew your first breath, then you are moving by His will. While it may not always appear so, there is direction and meaning in your life.

Think back over periods in your life when you thought you were moving one way and God brought you another way. Only He could have placed our feet on higher ground when many of us were traveling along self-destructive paths. Why does God move us and change our lives? It is all related to your purpose. He brought you to this point so you would hear what He has to say. You have purpose. God moves you for that purpose, so that you are prepared and in position to do His will.

When you "move into" your purpose, understand that God has called you to greater service, greater responsibility, greater sensitivity, greater love, and greater commitment (John 14:12). When God gives you the authority to utilize your talents and efforts in His name, recognize that it simply means He has placed you in the stead of Jesus Christ. You are God's representative on earth, according to

2 Corinthians 5: 20. We must move into our purpose because He imparts us life. This life is the Word of God. And, because He has saved us and blessed us, it is our responsibility to bless others, whether they are saved or unsaved.

There is a special role reserved for you, and God has equipped you to handle it. He has empowered you so that you can excel in the area of life that invokes all your passion. As you grow in Christ, an aspect of that growth involves discovering who He is in your life. After you are comfortable with His role, you will discover what your unique purpose is for this world. And, if you have not yet learned what that is, be confident that you do have one.

Christ simply wants to have a relationship with each one of us. Some people come to Him voluntarily, and others need examples to follow to come to Him. That is why you are so important as an instrument. What greater calling is there than to conduct our lives in such a way that we are vessels of His goodness? If He can utilize you in your purpose, then He has that many more saints to build His kingdom on earth.

We are given abundant opportunities to reside in His will. When we are less than we could be, Christ encourages us through His Word. He sends people of faith to guide us in our Christian walk. He embraces us with forgiveness and sends us out into the world with love. Christ wants us to maximize our potential because when we do so it glorifies Him. How could it not when He is the one who endowed us with our gifts and abilities? We are who we are only because of our personal relationship with Christ. We must pursue our purpose, not only for our own sake, but also for the good of mankind. He desires our self-actualization through the fulfillment of our dreams and our sense of joy at witnessing liberating changes in our lives. Christ wants you to maximize your potential. He only asks that you do so through Him.

Chapter Two

Developing Self-Confidence

"It is certain that our confidence rests more on the power of our relationship with Christ than the assumed importance of self."

It is important to understand our purpose in life; it is equally important to be able to walk in it. Moving into our purpose usually involves moving out of our comfort zones and thus becomes a transition that requires a degree of confidence. Confidence is critical because it ensures access to the people and places that are instrumental to our advancement. Thus, this self-assurance fills the void that your personal deficiencies may have created. Think about how difficult it is not to acknowledge people who walk with assurance. We all recognize this boldness of spirit whether it is expressed in the church, the workplace, or in our own homes.

While such people may be the same height as we are, they appear taller, more visible. They are unafraid to share who they are, while we fear exposing our personalities. We wonder what they possess that elevates them above the mundane. This elusive quality can transcend an individual from their very physical environment and certainly propel them into profundity of thought. Self-confidence is also recognized as an attribute that is common to all those who make the most of their abilities. Thus, our ability to maximize our potential depends on both understanding and possessing self-confidence.

For some Christians, it is a paradox to proclaim confidence in their relationship with Christ. This is because we are taught to humbly submit to His will. However, this very submission allows believers to receive a powerful gift. We receive the self-confidence as a result of a personal relationship with Christ. How does a relationship with Christ endow us with a quality that is essential to our success?

A prerequisite of being in Christ is that we are honest with ourselves. Whether in the physical world or in the spiritual realm, a relationship cannot be built or sustained on untruths. Thus, the need for truth is magnified when it comes to building a relationship with Christ. It is impossible to resist revealing ourselves to the One who knows us better than we do. Posturing in this way only hinders our efforts to create a more meaningful existence. Each of us desires to know Christ, whether that need is conscious or not. Our nature leads us to seek our Creator, and any rebellion against that reunion only impedes our growth. Christ simply waits for us to return to Him.

It is important that we be truthful in our relationship with Christ, which encourages us to be realistic about ourselves. Many people delude themselves concerning who they really are. They literally invent themselves because embracing their natural persona is either painful or disappointing. But, God had a purpose in creating each of us just the way we are. What you may perceive as a weakness, He will use to bless others.

When we assess ourselves honestly, we have begun a journey toward self-knowledge, which is the apparatus that molds our personalities and behavior to reflect Christ. When we know who we are, we are in a position to discover those talents, skills, abilities, and dreams in each of us that Christ develop and use will if only we submit them to His Lordship.

You have to acknowledge Christ as the originator of your potential. Scripture tells us that He created all things (John 1:3). It is also critical to understand that you will never maximize your potential if you are not seeking the glory of God. God has equipped us to do everything for His glory (1 Corinthians 10:38). This is important to understand because God can give you gifts, yet never give you opportunities to use those gifts if your focus is not on Him. Everyone knows the guy on the neighborhood basketball court who appears to have greater skills than the players with endorsements, but is relegated to the community park. Then, you see a professional player who may not have all the moves but testifies about how God allowed him to overcome insurmountable odds to play in the pros. God opens up opportunities for people He can use. A less talented player who acknowledges His presence is more effective for God than the more skilled one who never speaks of His grace.

This assessment of yourself and your abilities is necessary if you are to use your abilities effectively. Every day of your life, you need to know what you are capable of doing. You do not need to depend on anyone to tell you the amount of ability you have, that you are doing a good job, or that you have failed. God reveals that with which you are equipped, and offers opportunities to use your abilities. When you understand who you are, then you can work within your own parameters.

We need to be realistic about ourselves and accept who we are. Our power and ability becomes useless when we compare ourselves with others. When we want to be like others, we negate our own uniqueness. We also adopt every quality that those others possess, both positive and negative. Whether their weakness is visible or not, we know all of God's children are imperfect and have struggles. You have to know who you are and with what you have to work. The Lord wants you to address those things and become comfortable with the gifts He has allocated to you.

Examining our abilities for the purpose of being God's instrument is a demonstration of faith. Where He leads us is not always consistent with what the world says to do. Perhaps, you are being led into a trade that can be used for service, and people are telling you to attend a four-year college. But, we have to understand that college is not for everyone. We say it is, but it is not. It is great for those students who can attend and graduate. It is even greater when they can aspire to graduate from professional schools. But, if you are not led in that direction, assess your ability to do other things with your life that are just as worthwhile. Perhaps, a more realistic goal for you is to obtain some level of training and develop a skill. Do not concern yourself with what other people think of you. Learn how to utilize your skill extremely well, and the same people who criticized you will come to you for your services.

Every individual possesses potential, and discovering that potential is integral to understanding who you are. An adequate and realistic self-image leads to self-confidence. Without self-confidence, we are hampered in the essential actions of our lives. It does not matter how much you say, "I am going to do this," because if you do not believe you can do it, it will not be done. Furthermore, without belief in ourselves we are severely handicapped in reaching goals we have set for ourselves.

You will not maximize your potential if you do not believe you have any, because "...as he thinketh in his heart, so is he" (Proverbs 23:7a). This has nothing to do with the bravado you exhibit to the community. But, if in your innermost being there is not a strong belief in your abilities, it is as if God never endowed you with any. You cannot expand substance if you do not believe you have substance. You cannot expand power if you do not believe you have power. You cannot expand authority if you do not believe you have authority. The reality is that you have to accept these qualities as a valid part of yourself before you can utilize them.

The church and community have been robbed of true genius by a lack of self-confidence. Christians come into the church on fire, ready to go, and some little misguided person who has not felt the Spirit of God in years taps them on the shoulder and tells them, "The Lord is not requiring that of you; you don't have the ability for it." Be careful to whom you listen. One way you receive your faith is by what you hear (Romans 10:17a). God is a gentleman; He knows where you live. If He wants you to know something, He will go to your house and tell you. You want to become a doctor or lawyer, and someone tells you that the Lord told him or her that you could not do that. Who gave them that authority? If the Lord does not want you to become that, He will speak directly to you.

Perhaps, you are hindered by what people say to you. You are impressionable because you do not know for yourself who you are or what God is requiring of you. No consideration was given to the development of your inner self. People are too concerned with the appearance of the exterior, when it is the interior that garners the place in life that you desire. You allow people to speak to you about what you cannot do, and you believe they are speaking on some authority.

It is critical for your advancement that you develop self-confidence. Otherwise, other people will determine whom you can be rather than your having knowledge of whom God has called you to be. In the final analysis, not one of those persons is going to save your soul, and since they cannot do much for you, and cannot impart much knowledge or wisdom to you, why allow them to control your life?

Philippians 4:13 states "I can do all things through Christ which strengtheneth me." So, we have to put our focus in the right place. The Word says you can do all things through Christ, not through your friends or relatives. When your focus is right, other people are unable to control your life. Understand that when you are told you cannot do something in an area in which God has gifted you, oftentimes it is jealousy that is speaking. Do not let anyone discourage you from doing that which you know you can do.

It is the inner you who is most important, not the exterior. So, if you recognize that God places the most valuable part of you on the inside, then know that not everyone can see what you are capable of achieving through Christ. You have ability! God has given you ability, so put that in your mental repertoire and keep it there. The areas of ability are as varied as the individuals who have them. But, we all have the ability to do, to perform, to achieve and to succeed.

God has created you for a unique purpose. You are here for a divine reason; it may be that it simply has not been revealed to you yet. And, if you resist operating in His will, you cannot expect to experience the fullness of life He intended for you. That blessing is reserved for those whom Christ uses as instruments of His will. Because we often step out from under His covering, we struggle with a profound sense of emptiness and cannot understand why we are unfulfilled in life.

On the surface, we appear to have the best of jobs, earning a salary with just the right number of zeros. Our homes are showplaces with exquisitely decorated rooms. We have obtained the B.A., the M.A., the M.D., the Ph.D., and for some women the proper "Mrs." We drive luxury cars with plates reading "Blessed" and "Jesus Lives!" Yet inside, in a place to which our social circles are not privy, we are experiencing a feeling of dissatisfaction with our lives.

It is because we are not maximizing our potential in Christ. We were created to find our place in the bosom of Christ. And, when we are not there, whether due to rebellion or lack of understanding, we feel incomplete. Evidence of this cannot be found in your checking account or driveway. You can have earthly success without having spiritual prosperity. The evidence of this truth is found in your heart, where you face Christ alone and know you are not doing what He has called you to do.

Rather than submit to His call on their lives, some people have to go through hell before they understand that they always had access to heaven. If you are not operating in the position God intended for you, it is a fact that you will experience emptiness. And, no matter how many lovers you throw into your personal abyss, how much alcohol and how many drugs you use to forget that place within you, how much you try to hide your emptiness with weight, or cover it with the costume of happiness, or decorate it with the accumulation of goods, you will remain empty until you give yourself to Christ.

There are several qualities that keep us from maximizing our potential by contributing to our lack of self-confidence. The essence of this lack of self-confidence can be found in the deficiency of our relationship with Christ. Christians who are secure in their faith approach life with the assurance of God's promises. They believe good things will come to them as a result of their love and obedience, and thus they attract people and experiences of this nature. Those who are insecure in Christ are most often exposed in the pervasive qualities that erode their confidence level.

Indifference can nullify any move toward building self-confidence. People who exhibit this trait are incapable of pleasing God. This group lacks faith, and without faith, it is impossible to please God (Hebrews 11:6). They are too apathetic to concern themselves with any strong emotions concerning Him or the consequences of their attitude. God admonishes Christians to be either hot or cold, but He would spew out those who are lukewarm (Revelation 3:15-16).

The indifferent Christian is lukewarm and deserving only of God's contempt. Has He not shown you enough favor in your life to elicit a deeper response than indifference? It is impossible to imagine this individual caring enough to move himself where God would have him to be. Someone said, "A bread baked with indifference is a bitter bread, and feeds only half man's hunger," meaning that this level of response is an effrontery to its recipient.

Likewise, timid persons become ineffective at operating in their purpose because they lack the confidence to assert themselves. When God tells you your purpose and where He wants you to be, it is not necessarily a smooth process. On the contrary, you will meet your greatest opposition when you are moving in God's will. And, if Satan has not bothered you lately, you may want to reexamine what you are doing or not doing that is making him so comfortable. When you are in God's purpose for your life, Satan attacks because he wants you to believe you should follow what the world tells you to do. Satan knows that if he can achieve this, he has greater access to you and can manipulate you into resisting kingdom building. It is important to understand that opposition from Satan is an indication that you are moving in God's will, and that there is no room for timidity in this spiritual battle.

In the same vein, some Christians undermine their opportunity to excel in their abilities because they do not exercise their voice. They are literally too quiet to speak to others about their identity and their areas of giftedness. The danger here is that if they cannot share who they are, how can they share who Jesus is in the face of opposition? Self-confidence is rarely nurtured in silence. The very nature of self-confidence demands the enriching light of attention, the creative tending of prolific thoughts, and the aqueous attendance of a deliberate voice.

There are some Christians who are simply too "backward" to go forward in life. I am referring to those persons who cannot make confident efforts because they are not involved in progressive pursuits. They are not using their energy and intellect for the purpose of glorifying God. We have learned that self-confidence grows out of a positive relationship with Christ. If self-confidence were a gift given from Christ, why would He empower you to do other than that related to His business of kingdom building?

Confidence is not simply a buoy for when you are discouraged. Those persons who are easily discouraged do not understand this because confidence is a foreign concept. They are told they cannot do a particular thing and they give up. Have you ever known such a person? Have you ever been so easily discouraged that you were swayed from your objective by a breath of criticism? It is nearly impossible to live as a Christian and not be subject to some level of persecution. The Word of God clearly states in 1 Corinthians 4:12 that persecution will come to us. We only need to know how to handle it. And, in that experience, you must remember that you are being persecuted for Jesus' sake. For Him, you should consider standing up for what you believed in the moment before you allowed someone to deny you that.

It is folly to allow those who do not know what God has placed within you and do not really "see" you to tell you who you are. That authority is reserved for Christ. You must let people know that you are not afraid of them. Sometimes, people may appear larger than you because your confidence level is lower than that of your opposition, but you have to learn to go beyond that. In other words, no one and nothing is allowed to hinder you from reaching your goal.

Some people consciously contribute to a lack of confidence because they despair of ever experiencing change. Many times these people set themselves up for disappointment because they desire change without bestirring themselves to actually change the situation. They offer a pensive prayer, and then like a child at Christmas, expect a miraculous alteration in their relationships, finances, emotions and lifestyle. God is not a genie to be called on and then put away when He does not produce according to our time frames. History attests to the fact that He prefers to test the "cafeteria" Christian, a professing Christian who believes he can pick and choose the components of the Christian life that are convenient for his lifestyle.

Others may be discontent with their lives, but not enough to fight back. Rather than prove to themselves and others that they can succeed, they validate their low self-esteem by continuing to exist in an unsatisfactory manner. The irony is that if they exhibited a level of confidence consistent with their blessings, they would enjoy a higher quality of life.

People who too often expect disappointment receive it. Remember, faith is the substance of things hoped for (Hebrew 11:1). Don't you know you are going to fail if you expect to fail? If you start a project and expect it not to go well, you are already defeated. If you walk into a job interview believing you are not going to get the job because of the way you look, your gender, etc., then guess what? You will not get the job — not because of your imagined failings, but because you claimed defeat in advance. Whenever you are in a situation where you are discontented, you need to learn how to address it.

If you are going to maximize your potential, you will have to think in terms of what you are going to do. Then, you must think about how successful you are going to be; you must think in a positive manner. You can do anything you want to do. It may take a long time to get it done, but you can do it! Did you know that change comes about because somebody was dissatisfied with the way things were (status quo)? Somebody got tired of riding horses, so the change they inspired resulted in cars. It is the same with all the advancements in the world, so why should the changes in our lives not be motivated in like manner?

What if you are a person who lacks self-confidence? Then, you must reassess your worth as a human being and recognize that your true value comes from a relationship with Christ. If He accepts you, then you have good reason to be confident about yourself. You are a person with intellect, ability, substance and power. If you know from being in Christ and His being in you that you possess these attributes, then maximize them with self-confidence! It makes no difference to Christ whom you were or even whom you are today. Through Him, you can be the best in whatever endeavor you choose, because you can do all things through Him (Philippians 4:13). Say to the world, "I am here and I am a force with which to be reckoned!" Proclaim, "Twenty-five qualified people are going after this one position, but I am going to get it!" Claim the wholeness of your family, the binding of your marriage, the prosperity of your finances, and the ability to maximize in Jesus' name, and believe it done.

Lack of self-confidence is commonly a result of dealing with self-doubt. Observation and experience tend to support five areas in which self-doubt hinder the development of an individual's developing self-confidence. A particularly impactive area is when individuals come under heavy criticism; it fosters self-doubt, because they begin to question their ability. "How can I be effective in this position if everyone sees my shortcomings?"

If God has placed you in a position that you know you could not have attained alone, then trust that He has also given you the tools necessary to accomplish the task. Proverbs 23:7a states, "For as he thinketh in his heart, so is he." A person must think they are able in order to display evidence of being so. In like fashion, if you make a person think they cannot do a thing, they will not do anything.

As parents, we have to be very careful with criticism of our children. It is detrimental to their well-being to constantly critic the nuggets of encouragement, and then offer some options for improvement. Is that not how Christ moves us to ameliorate our condition?

The same methods apply in the church family. Somebody just got appointed over a little group and they may not have found their rhythm yet, but everyone is so critical. They may not do it your way, but they can get the job done. The people with whom you deal should be encouraged to think positively, not negatively, about what they are doing. Consider how you would want others to respond to you in a new situation. Would criticism or encouragement be more effective in helping you maximize your potential?

Taking on too much responsibility too soon is another experience that can create self-doubt. Society says that our standing in the world is often measured by the amount of responsibility we have. But, it is possible to give a person too much responsibility before they have matured to a point where they can handle it. If a young person feels called to minister at Wednesday night service, and you pressure him to speak at Men's Day the following Sunday, he is destined to fail. This would not help him, and the next time he got up in front, he would feel uncomfortable. People have to be groomed to receive the responsibility of certain positions; otherwise, you are orchestrating a script for self-doubt and certain disaster.

When you are not prepared, it is certain you will question yourself in that experience. What is the point of desiring to do a task when you have not properly prepared yourself? For example, if there is a meeting called in the church or workplace, whoever is in charge of the meeting should come prepared. What impression of the organization or task is created when the leader is uncertain about what issues to address? "What are we going to discuss when we get there?" "Oh, I don't know, we'll come up with something when we all get together."

Prepare yourself so that you are credible and have the knowledge to handle that situation. Paul was prepared before Jesus called him. He did not get prepared after he was called; he was prepared before the call. If you want to be a preacher or missionary someday, you must study the Word of God now. The value of preparation is that when your opportunity opens up, you can apply your efforts to it immediately. You must prepare to maximize your potential!

Another area where people allow self-doubt to affect their belief in their abilities is a natural impediment or handicap. I Samuel 16:7b states, "...the LORD seeth not as man seeth; for man looketh on the outward appearance, but the LORD looketh on the heart." Is it not a relief to know that when God passed out potential, He looked at the best part of us (i.e., the heart)? So, do not allow any aspect of your physical body or speech to discourage you from doing what you know you can do. You will continue to experience doubt when you place your hope in people because they do not always have the vision to see beyond your image. But, when God lovingly created you with differences, it was still with the emphasis on fulfilling your purpose.

Loss of self-respect through sin is one of the most impacting experiences that erodes confidence. Now, if you have not been doing what you should in the Lord, you do not always feel like praying because it is unclear whether or not He is going to answer. "Well, Lord, after you get through forgiving me for everything, then please grant my request." But, you can have confidence when you have a good relationship with the Lord. You can increase your self-confidence through new birth, which brings with it renewed potential for self-esteem and, thus, confidence.

I John 3:2a teaches us why we should be confident: "Beloved, now are we the sons of God, and it doth not yet appear what we shall be...." Earlier in our Christian walk, we may have understood this text to refer to Jesus coming back to earth, at which time we would be changed from mortal to immortal being. But, we are the children of God because we are in His spirit, and "...when He shall appear, we shall be like Him" (I John 3:2b). This will not occur on Judgment Day, but at His appearing. When Christ appears before us to become a part of us, we shall be like Him in spirit. If God is omnipotent and has all the confidence in the world, and He lives in us, then where should our confidence be?

The reason we are so confident in the new birth and being born again is because our spirit has been changed and enhanced with His presence. And, this very presence, which cannot be compromised or controlled, enables us to confront whatever is before us and proclaim ourselves to be victorious. God never approached His ability to do anything in a hesitant manner, and if that same Spirit resides within you, then you will approach things in like manner.

Genesis 1:27 states, "So, God created man in His own image, in the image of God He created him; male and female He created them." Although Adam failed, Jesus brought about reconciliation, so that we are no longer destined to the sinful nature of Adam but are transformed into the image of Christ. It follows that, if we are in His image, then we also share in His attributes, which should elicit some degree of change in our lives. As a child of God, you should be able to respond correctly to the events in your life because you have been empowered with the spirit of Christ.

"And if children, then heirs; heirs of God, and joint-heirs with Christ; if so be that we suffer with him, that we may be also glorified together" (Romans 8:17). Essentially this means that if you are an heir of God, you should have good self-esteem and a positive image of yourself. The Word informs us that we are joint heirs, so whatever Christ has, we have. The Spirit that is in Him is also in us. You can maximize your potential with confidence because your confidence is not in your own mental faculties, but in the Spirit of the Lord.

We should be further encouraged in our quest to maximize our potential by understanding I Peter 2:9: "But ye are a chosen generation, a royal priesthood, an holy nation, a peculiar people; that ye should show forth the praises of Him who hath called you out of darkness into His marvellous light." We are recognized as a people with unique qualities. So, as we come to discover our true identity through the Word of God, we can begin fulfilling our purpose today. God has prepared you so that you can have the confidence you need to go out there and get what you want.

If you want it, go get it! Nothing you desire is going to fall from the sky. In times past, saints used to testify about how they would go outside when it rained and see dollars floating in the water along the curb. You will not see too many dollars floating today. And, if they were to start at the other end of the block, someone would get them before they floated down to you. So, do not count on the elements. If you want to maximize your potential, you have to do it yourself. Ephesians 2:10 says, "For we are His workmanship, created in Christ Jesus unto good works, which God hath before ordained that we should walk in them." We can maximize our potential because we have been created and energized for it. We have the ability to produce and so we need to start doing.

Nobody is going to encourage you until you affirm yourself. God has already equipped you to do His works, so you just have to overcome the negatives in your life. Shake off those negative influences. If people are putting you down, speak to them right there. You have to talk to people and let them know whom you are — be strong. Self-confidence grows out of competence. It is not a cosmetic, used to cover your face, because when you get through, you are still the same person. Whatever you do, you are yet that person when you remove the facade of confidence.

Self-confidence has deep roots in our spirit; it is the outflowing of strength that comes from within. It comes from the soul, so it is not what someone says that makes you who you are; your individuality is based on what God has placed inside of you. If you want to succeed, success is within you. If you want to be strong, strength is there. Whatever you want to be, it is within you. You have the potential and all you need to do is maximize it. Allow your potential to have its reign every day of your life. Get up in the morning knowing that you are special. Get up as if the whole earth exists because of you.

This kind of confidence has no relationship to conceit; rather it is working realistically within the parameters you have. If you have not attended medical school, then being a doctor is not for you, no matter how much con you can excel.

God is on our side. It is not necessary to call Him down from a high place, because He is with you. Always feel confident that the Lord is with you, because He promised in Hebrew 13:5b, "I will never leave thee, nor forsake thee." God remains with you in trouble or stress, during a job interview, on your sick bed, while driving your car, wherever you are. No one but the Lord will show such faithfulness and love to you, so express your gratitude by confidently walking in His will.

Since you are special in His sight, He will not allow any temptation to come your way that is too great (1 Corinthians 10:13). You can overcome any temptation, because in the spirit you have already prevailed. It should make little difference how difficult it may seem, because you have the grace and confidence for every task and responsibility that He gives you.

It is time to maximize our potential, and if we want something, we are going to get it. If it is more joy, we are getting it; more peace, we are getting it;

more love, we are getting it. Whether our needs are for tranquility, stability in our finances, stronger relationships, positive attitudes, whatever, we are getting it. And, we are telling the devil to get out of our way because we are coming through with self-confidence.

As we consider the essential elements of developing our self-confidence, it becomes clear that our responsibility is to implement them into our daily life. We can develop our self-confidence to the greatest extent by focusing on our relationship with Christ. When we seek to know Him better, He in turn shows us who we are in Him. And, the reflection of ourselves in Christ is a completely different image than what the world reveals to us.

Our assurance rests on the knowledge that we are in Christ and He in us. While society perceives confidence as an individual's response to himself, we are renewed with the knowledge that it comes from a greater source than man. If confidence were simply a reaction to external forces it would be subject to the fluctuation of emotions and experiences. But, since it is the result of a shared relationship with Christ, then every Christian has the opportunity to embrace this quality. And, Christ further validates us, in that, this gift does more than enhance our emotional well being; it also inspires us to a greater exercise of our potential.

Chapter Three

Accomplishing the Impossible

"The caterpillar is God's spokesman on maximizing one's potential."

I f we are to maximize our potential, we must not allow our confidence to be eroded by the pressures of life. Rather, we must exhibit strength in the problem areas of our lives. We have to reevaluate the way we perceive problems in our Christian journey. Each problem should be viewed as something that supports us. Remember, all things work together for our good (Romans 8:28).

This essentially means that we should gain experience from going through difficulties and apply it to our daily living. A problem should not be viewed as an invasion that has the power to weaken us.

Experiencing problems should be an exercise that strengthens us. Every time you go through a problem, it serves as a vehicle for developing your spiritual stamina. This is so that nothing is taken away from your total person every time you go through a difficult situation. Jesus never allowed anything to cause Him to be less than who He was. He was the Son of God, independent of worldly pressures. He was the Son of God even in the midst of pressures.

In modeling ourselves after Christ, we should examine how He faced ungodly influences and maintained His integrity. Jesus justified us through His Word. And, when we accepted His sanctification and adoption, we became sons and daughters of God. We have been placed in a special position in Him because we are His chosen people. And, He chose us so that we might represent Him here on earth as a powerful force, not as weaklings broken by the impact of obstacles.

Romans 8:37 declares, "Nay, in all these things we are more than conquerors through Him that loved us." As we enter into the spiritual battles that wear the guise of problems, we must battle with confidence, with force, and with the thought that we cannot be defeated. As a matter of fact, we battle by faith, knowing that in the Spirit we have already won. But, that victory must be manifested in the flesh so that what was can exist in the present.

The prerequisite to maximizing our potential is to have faith in God. It is critical that we look not to our flesh and understanding, but that we operate in the Spirit. "Have faith in God," Jesus said in Mark 11:22. He goes on to say, "For verily I say unto you, That whosoever shall say unto this mountain, 'Be thou removed, and be thou cast into the sea;' and shall not doubt in his heart, but shall believe that those things which he saith shall come to pass; he shall have whatsoever he saith. Therefore I say unto you, What things soever ye desire, when ye pray, believe that ye receive them, and ye shall have them" (Mark 11:23-24).

It is important that we learn to confess the faith that we have, for the lack of confessing usually indicates an area of doubt. Doubt tends to erode our confidence. And, if confidence is an indication of a right relationship with Christ, and we are experiencing doubt, then what does that say about our relationship with Him? Why would you share a testimony if you were not secure about its validity? But, if you are convinced that God's Word holds truths for you and that you can accomplish what you will, you will speak about it.

God has given us the opportunity to witness miracles, and this guarantees the occurrence of impossible things. But, you must first have faith that God will do it. Recognize that His ability to do great things does not rely on fluctuating human faith. Whether you have faith or not, He will do what He promised. All His promises are sure (1 Corinthians 1:20). So, whether you believe it or not, He will do it because He is God. He has already demonstrated His ability to perform by creating the earth out of nothing. When you examine the annals of human history, whether Biblical or secular, you will find evidence of the power of God.

What does having faith in the Lord mean? It means that where you are in your faith indicates where you are in your relationship with Him. Romans 1:17b declares, "The just shall live by faith." That is to say, there is an absentia from the flesh and the workings of your mental faculties to moving you to such a level in the spirit that you understand faith differently. You will begin to realize that the faith you have is not the faith that you have developed yourself because of past experiences. Rather this renewal of faith comes from the knowledge that you are a part of Him and He of you.

The Word of God says, "If ye abide in Me, and My words abide in you, ye shall ask what ye will, and it shall be done unto you" (John 15:7). Accepting this concept requires that you move away from your own thought processes and into the thoughts of God. When you move into the will of God, you have the faith of God because the will of God is the Word of God and the Word performs for God. John 1:1 & 3b states, "In the beginning was the Word, and the Word was with God and the Word was God.... and without him was not any thing made that was made."

So, when you move into the Word of God, you have the faith of God and thus are able to perform seemingly impossible feats. Some Christians fear we are moving close to heresy when we say we have the faith of God. But, if you have any faith, it must be His faith. While we exhibit various levels of faith, only divine faith will always work because it acts on the Word of God.

If you have the degree of faith that He has, then tell me what can come against you? God already let us know that He is the only God and that there is none beside Him. So, if He is God, what is too hard for Him? Since He is the Creator and everything came from Him, can He not control all things? When one reflects on His vastness, His majesty, His creativity, it is amazing that this Supreme Being will also empower to succeed in your endeavors.

Whatever you need to help you live, if it is not already made, He will create it for you. God will speak to the mind of someone to create that, which will provide for your needs. Mark 11:23 says, "For verily I say unto you, that whosoever shall say unto this mountain...." We look at this scripture and think of the improbability of using our voice to move a mountain, and yet the Lord says it will move. Faith means knowing that if that mountain is hindering your spiritual progress, it will be moved. If it is a barrier to the salvation of man, it will be moved. If it will save a nation, it will be moved. While this scripture does not refer to a literal mountain, it does apply to the mountains in our lives — although God can move any literal mountain He desires. And, He will accomplish even that through us, if necessary.

There is a condition we need to meet and that is releasing doubt from our hearts. Once that is accomplished, we can move to a position of believing. The Word talks about how the double-minded person will not receive anything. Nothing will be given to someone with a doubting spirit. God wants you to be receptive to what His spirit is doing in your life.

Mark 11: 25 says, "And when ye stand praying, forgive, if ye have ought against any: that your Father also which is in heaven may forgive you your trespasses." To maximize your potential, you must "clean the slate" and clear your conscience. If you have anything in your heart against somebody, you cannot flow in the Spirit. And, if you are not in the spirit, then the word of God cannot affect you, and you cannot exercise faith. Have you ever been talking to God and your communication was clouded by some sin, whether of commission or omission? You try to free your mind of these things and then find yourself asking for forgiveness. You should be exercising faith, but you cannot because you are exercising repentance.

Guilt is a great hindrance to miracles because forgiveness has not yet been bestowed. To be free to move in the spirit, one must have received forgiveness. "For God so loved the world, that He gave his only begotten Son, that whosoever believeth in Him should not perish, but have everlasting life" (John 3:16). The purpose of Christ's ultimate sacrifice was to offer us forgiveness. And, through forgiveness of sin we can move into that place where we can exercise the power of God. He wants us to enter into that place so He can work through us. The power He has ordained for us should be evident in every aspect of our lives.

The purpose of the Holy Ghost as the executive of the Godhead is to be an agent on this earth, living with us to empower us. That is why He is here. There are some Christians who believe that when you receive the Holy Ghost at conversion, you never lose any of the Spirit attributes that you receive. That is not true. You have to implore the Holy Spirit to operate in your life through the process of Christian maturation. If you buy a new car but never give it proper maintenance, how long do you suppose you will drive it?

What has this to do with our salvation? Acts 2:4 says, "And they were all filled with the Holy Ghost, and began to speak with other tongues, as the Spirit gave them utterance." The disciples received the power of the Holy Ghost, and then they went out into the field and talked about Jesus, lifting up His name. As they preached about Him, the officials and the magistrates become upset with them because they were preaching that Jesus Christ was the source of deliverance and power. As punishment, the disciples were beaten and talked about.

At this point they could have thrown in the towel and surrendered to the civic authorities. They could have taken the easy route and concluded that the promulgation of the Gospel was too costly. They did not choose any of those options because they had faith. The Word of God says that they went again into the upper room and stayed there until they received a refilling of the Holy Ghost. In like manner, we must determine that our initial encounter with the Holy Spirit does not provide us with an endless resource of strength and power. As we mature in Christ, we come to realize that we will be tested continually by Satan and must on occasion seek a refilling of the Holy Ghost.

The thing that motivated the disciples to seek another encounter with the Holy Spirit was the intensity of the storm they had endured. They were weakened by the work they had done for the Lord, so they needed to have a spiritual "refilling" to resume witnessing. You had better believe that from time to time you will need to have the Holy Ghost rekindled within you. The anointing of God moving within you is the only thing that will enable you to stand firm consistently. Occasionally, you need to try to increase that level of maturity in the Lord. It is only through growth and maturation that you are able to have the faith necessary to maximize your potential!

Part of the maturation process is learning how to forgive your brother or sister in Christ. If someone wronged you, sometimes it takes awhile to be reconciled to that person. Yes, healing is a process, but it is necessary if you are going to move forward in the excellence that God desires for your life. Or, you may recognize that you are the source of someone else's pain. We have all done something that does not fully measure up to God.

First, you must go to them and forgive them (or ask for their forgiveness). Let them know, "Yes, you hurt my feelings; yes, you hurt me, but I forgive you." Then, once you have extended the hand of forgiveness you must rejoice with that person. Healing will begin to take place as you rejoice. This does not imply that all of the pain is gone but is an expectancy that God will bring about complete deliverance. There is victory in the fact that once again you are able to fellowship in love with that brother or sister and that there is nothing that is hindering Christ from moving in your life.

Sometimes, husbands and wives live in the same house but sleep in different rooms because they have no unity. They come to church and fellowship together and on the surface appear to be unified. They pray and seek the Lord's face diligently, but they are not hearing from God. Prayers will not be answered until the wall between them is broken. Since two cannot walk together unless they are in agreement (Amos 3:3), the couple must get rid of that partition and experience the oneness, which comes with forgiveness and repentance. You cannot justify your attitude by the circumstances. "Well, Lord, you know that Sister Suzy deserves the cold shoulder because of the way she spoke to me last Sunday." Until there is freedom from bitterness and resentment, there will be no mountain-moving miracle in your life. In order for miracles to occur, there cannot be jealousy or anger in your heart. Miracles will happen only as you commit your will to forgiveness.

A Christian should feel explosiveness, that spiritual dynamo that man-child on the inside stirring and causing growth everywhere. One should feel and hear God saying, "You can do the impossible, for with Me nothing is impossible." We are told in Philippians 4:13, "I can do all things through Christ which strengtheneth me." It is Christ who gives us the ability to move the mountains in our lives. As we learn to exercise forgiveness, God rewards us with a testimony of His power in our lives.

Once we receive that testimony, we can go out and witness to the lost. We can tell them, "I know that you are in bondage and in need of relief, and I know somebody who can help you." He is not Buddha or Confucius or any other "god" who was born and died. He is the only God who rose from the grave with all power in His hands! This Jesus Christ is alive and changed me from who I was to who I am by His power. It is through Him that I have become a force to be reckoned with. I have the authority and power to take control of my life and I can prove it to you. Then, you list those things that

Christ has enabled you to do through him. After sharing your testimony, you invite that person to come and meet Christ.

One of the greatest revivals recorded in the Bible happened through a woman to whom most of us would not ever speak or acknowledge. The Book of John states that Jesus had reason to go through Samaria because there was a city that needed saving and He had to talk to someone. In His weariness from travel, He rested by a well and here is where we come to understand that Christ offers us forgiveness to free us from the burden of guilt that hinders growth.

John 4:7 states, "There cometh a woman of Samaria to draw water: Jesus saith unto her, 'Give Me to drink.'" Jesus knew who she was and what her response would be before He approached her. The significant thing is that He acknowledges her. Then, He gives her an opportunity to respond to Him by either operating in His will or choosing not to. Christ asks us for things in our life as well, already knowing our resources and of what we are capable.

In verse 9, the Samaritan woman says to Him, "How is it that Thou, being a Jew, askest drink of me, which am a woman of Samaria? For the Jews have no dealings with the Samaritans." Her response was based on the cultural facts of the time. How many distinctions do we make in society, even today, that distances us from others? Yet, God reveals in His Word that He is no respecter of persons, and this is one of the most powerful lessons in this scripture. If God can make use of those relegated to the margins of society to teach us about His character, then who are we to disassociate ourselves from them?

We are not privy to God's perspective on man and cannot understand how He continuously utilizes the most unlikely subjects for His purpose. See, His thoughts and ways are higher than ours (Isaiah 55:8-9). So, while you continue in your Christian conceit because you head the usher board and lead a prayer group, the Lord will bypass you because of the true state of your spirit. Then, He will take that new member who just came out of the world and whose name no one knows and elevates them beyond you because they are a greater testimony to His goodness.

Jesus answers her beginning in verse 10, "If thou knewest the gift of God, and who it is that saith to thee, 'Give Me to drink;' thou wouldest have asked of Him, and He would have given thee living water.... Whosoever drinketh of this water shall thirst again: But, whosoever drinketh of the water that I shall give him shall never thirst; but the water that I shall give him shall be in him a well of water springing up into everlasting life." The blessing of living in Christ's will is that, when we respond to Him, He offers us more than we could imagine. In exchange for her obedience in giving Him a drink of water, He will give her eternal life. How can we not serve such a God?

When the Samaritan woman asked to receive the living water, Jesus told her to go and bring her husband back. She then told Jesus that she had no husband. In John 4:17-18, Jesus said to her, "Thou hast well said, 'I have no husband': For thou hast had five husbands; and he whom thou now hast is not thy husband: in that saidst thou truly." Some people say that He meant that the man belonged to someone else, but that is not what Jesus was saying. The man was not her husband. She had told the truth: she had gotten rid of all the others; they were not hers.

Those of you who are divorced need to think again about meddling in your spouses' lives. You are upset because your wife or husband got remarried; it is best if you divert your energy and attention elsewhere. After you have divorced a person and that person remarries, they are no longer yours and you need to leave them alone. Although the Bible says you are married until death part you, understand that God never intended for there to be divorce, God granted Moses a bill of divorce only because of the hardness of the human heart.

Once the divorce is final, that is the end of it. This is important for someone who has not moved on emotionally. You cannot maximize your potential if you are living in the past; still trying to hurt that person you have not yet forgiven. Instead of focusing on what you have lost, look at what you have left. You have got to live in the now. And, if God is going to work in your life, He is going to do it today.

So, those husbands of the Samaritan woman were gone, and the man she was with was not hers. She marveled at the fact that Jesus knew. He knows everything about us. He has this knowledge because He created all things. He knew before the woman got married that she would do so. He knew before she met the men that she would meet them. He knew before she walked away that she would walk away. Most importantly, He knew she would be at the well, and that is why He went there. There is nothing that Christ does not know; there is nothing that He does not understand. He is omniscient! The Samaritan woman got excited when Christ revealed whom she was! Sometimes, when the Lord deals with us about where we are, instead of getting excited and changing our lives, we run and hide. This woman did not hide; she did not look miserable. He did something for her that she needed.

When your past is haunting you, when the past is hindering your progress, when you have been wallowing in obscurity and hiding in the darkness because of something you have done, you have to trust Christ enough to come out of that obscurity. Every once in a while you need the light to shine on you so you can see where you are. Then, you will know that God is a forgiving God. He will forgive you no matter what you have done in your life. There are no big sins and little sins; all unrighteousness is sin. Any transgression of the law is sin, so it does not matter what you have done.

Whatever you have done, it is in the past. And, to maximize your potential, you must release the pain and guilt of your past. Somebody said they robbed somebody; that was yesterday. Another person said they committed adultery — that was yesterday. Still another said that they murdered someone; that was yesterday as well. Stop thinking about how terrible you have been and thank God for the righteousness you find in yourself today.

We have all made some wrong decisions in our lives. You have done it, the Samaritan woman did it! But, here comes the light of the world, here is hope and help speaking to her. Here is a man who offers her religious tranquility. Here is a man who offers her a greater gift than all her worldly husbands ever could: eternal life. She gets excited, and verses 28-29 tells us, "The woman then left her waterpot, and went her way into the city, and saith to the men, 'Come, see a man, which told me all things that ever I did: is not this the Christ?'" She urged them to see a Man who was spectacular and special.

How did the woman know He was spectacular and special? Because, He told her everything she had ever done. She took a moment of defeat and turned it around. She took truth, which may not appear to be much to some, and she maximized that truth. She told everyone she came into contact with about the truth, and the whole city came out to hear what Jesus had to say.

One Samaritan woman brought a city to repentance and a proclamation of faith in Jesus. In John 4:42, the city people said, "Now we believe, not because of thy saying: for we have heard Him ourselves, and know that this is indeed the Christ, the Saviour of the world." She maximized the truth that Jesus shared with her to bring about one of the greatest recorded revivals in the Bible. What could we accomplish for Christ if we also shared our testimony with the world?

We can accomplish that which seems impossible. How do we do it? I John 4:4 says, "Ye are of God, little children, and have overcome them: because greater is He that is in you, than he that is in the world." The Christian believer, because he has the Holy Spirit living in him, has power over all things! Where do we get it? We are empowered by Jesus. How can we exercise it? By having faith and not doubting in our hearts. Also, by both accepting and offering forgiveness so that our souls can be set free.

How many of you know that if you hold on to hostility, hurt, and disappointment it will cause you to pass on the same experiences to others? God does not work through negativity, but through creativity. If you have resolved that you can do all things through Christ who strengthens you, you will be able to do it. There is no demon anywhere who is stronger than you are. Not financial demon, romantic demon, platonic demon, no demon can attack your children, your spouse, or your job who is more powerful than you are. The reason you are so strong is because of the force of God inside of you.

When God is inside you, the devil has no option but to recognize His presence. Satan is not dissuaded by your articulateness and eloquence or by your rhetorical exercises. But, He does acknowledge the power you have in Jesus' name. In Luke 9, Jesus empowers the disciples with what He has. If He gave this power to the Twelve, we also are recipients of that same power. "Then He called his twelve disciples together, and gave them power and authority over all devils, and to cure diseases. And, He sent them to preach the kingdom of God, and to heal the sick" (Luke 9:1-2).

When Jesus transferred His power to them, they did not have to believe they were going to have it; they did not have to beg for it. The mere fact that Jesus gave power to them meant they automatically had power over Satan. Why? Because, the power He gave them was His power and His power is greater than that of Satan. You do not have to get on your knees to beg God for more power. Power comes because He wants you to have it. Do you not know Christ intends for us to subdue Satan and his demonic influences in His name? He wants us to have the tools to protect our families and overcome ungodly forces.

The disciples were amazed that even the demons were subject to them in Jesus' name. But, Jesus admonished them not to rejoice in this, but to rejoice because their names were written in heaven. In like manner, we should be glad because if we are saved, then our names are also written in heaven. If your name is written in heaven, there is an exchange between His name and your name, and you receive power of attorney. Then, heaven knows you can use the name of Jesus wherever you go because your name is authenticated. You can say, "In the name of Jesus, be thou removed" to every situation in life. "Mountain, get out of my way in the name of Jesus." The body is healed in the name of Jesus. The spirit is lifted in the name of Jesus. Wrong becomes right in the name of Jesus.

If your name is written in heaven, you have unlimited authority over every experience and spirit in your life. While Satan will constantly attack you,

you can stand firm in the knowledge that you have unlimited authority over him. You can resist his influences entirely. God has given you power to fight successfully. If you fail in spiritual battle, it is because your lacked faith, not because you did not have power to win.

Were you disappointed today? There will be more of that tomorrow. Lost some money today? You can count on losing more tomorrow. Feelings got hurt today? They are going to get hurt tomorrow. But, the power that has been given to you by Jesus will function as an energizing force to help you overcome the problem. The power that you have will conquer all difficulties, because in the name of Jesus you can accomplish the impossible.

The authority and power you have is nothing compared to that which resides in heaven. Can you imagine being able to talk to Jesus? Can you imagine being able to talk to God because your name is officially registered? You can just say, "Jesus, I need to talk to You. I'm going through some changes in my life and I need You to walk with me." He has already said in His Word, "Yea, though I walk through the valley of the shadow of death, I will fear no evil, for Thou art with me; Thy rod and Thy staff, they comfort me" (Psalms 23:4).

How do you know that He is with you? Because, your name is written in heaven and His Spirit dwells within you. Whatever the circumstances, you have the power in you to handle them.

You have substance, ability, power, and authority. You know that you possess these attributes because God is with you wherever you go. He will be your doctor, your lawyer, your way maker, your heart fixer, and your mind regulator. Christ is in you, and He will move the obstacles of your life and subdue satanic forces. This is so that, no matter what you can maximize your potential for His glory.

You have unlimited authority and ability. That knowledge should act as an impetus for accomplishing those goals you have set. And, our alliance with Christ ensures that we can conquer obstacles in our path. Nothing is too hard for God. And, because God lives in you and you acquiesce to His power, there is nothing too hard for you. The impossible becomes possible through Christ!

• **Maximize Your Potential** •

Chapter Four

Change Through Christ

"It is unfortunate that people believe that change is merely substituting a worldly mask for a spiritual one."

One of the most empowering concepts associated with accomplishing the impossible through Christ is that it involves change. The ability to change is critical to Christian living. This change is most often reflected in our spirit, behavior and speech. It can be extended to our relationships, our jobs and within our areas of interest. The ability to change is not limited only to ourselves, but can be communicated to others so that their lives are transformed, as well. We simply need to move to a level in God where we can exercise to the fullest extent the power we have within us. We have tremendous power to change things within our lives. While it may initially seem fearful to some, the truth is that all of us are desirous of change.

Everyone wants to do better than they are presently doing. This desire is in all of us, but the areas in which change is needed vary. We all desire, to some extent, more financial prosperity so that we can have a degree of stability. One may yearn for better health so that their body allows them greater mobility. For another it may be closer relationships with family and friends, while the next person may only desire more opportunities to achieve something in their life. "Better" means different things to different people. Yet, there is nothing wrong in wanting to rise above our current situation and improve our lot.

How do we mobilize change in our lives? You have found yourself in the same place year after year and are uncertain how to change your situation. You have always wanted something different; you have even presented your case before the Lord, but to no avail. It is not that God did not answer you; He has already given you what you need to change your life (2 Peter 1:3). You simply have not received His power within your spirit.

We invoke change in our lives through God's power. It is the force that we need to move the stubbornly static conditions of our lives. Since we are heirs of God's attributes, we can appropriate His power and move in it. And, since our power is from God, we are imbued with the ability to grow and change. Once you understand that you have Christ's power, what can prevent you from changing certain aspects of yourself? Who will stop you from assuming a greater sense of identity in Christ? Who can hinder you from being reborn? Who will obstruct your salvation, that is, if the power in which you are moving is from God?

When you are empowered with the Spirit of God, Satan is forced to recognize it, as well. He knows that Christ has already defeated him and that if you are in Christ, you have the same power over Him. This is a truth on which we need to hold, because when Satan attacks — and he will — you need to know that you can repel those attacks. So, many Christians allow Satan to disrupt their homes, their marriages, and their sense of peace and all without fighting back. "Oh, Satan is beating me from pillar to post. The devil is ruining my life." When you do not fight back, you are essentially giving Satan permission to cause disorder.

Being a Christian does not protect you from being attacked by the enemy. It actually invites the advances of Satan, because his goal is to tear down the kingdom of God. But, God has given you everything you need to defend yourself. Ephesians 6:13-17 states:

Wherefore take unto you the whole armour of God, that ye may be able to withstand in the evil day, and having done all, to stand. Stand therefore, having your loins girt about with truth, and having on the breastplate of righteousness; And your feet shod with the preparation of the gospel of peace; Above all, taking the shield of faith, wherewith ye shall be able to quench all the fiery darts of the wicked. And take the helmet of salvation, and the sword of the Spirit, which is the Word of God.

Do you prepare yourself every day to do battle? Satan is ready to attack you every opportunity he gets, and if you are not prepared, even for one day, he will seek to destroy you.

God tells us how to preserve our spirits against Satan. He does so because, unlike us, He is aware of Satan's purpose on earth. That purpose is to destroy all who believe in God (John 10:10a). Our surprise at being attacked proves that we are not truly aware of Satan's goal. Church people are always surprised and hurt by Satan's attempts to hinder them. Why? That is what Satan does. You are so hurt that someone is lying to you, another person is slandering your good name, and Satan has moved another person to impede your promotion. You should not be surprised by Satan doing his job on earth. If we were more focused on Christ, we could better prepare a stronger counter-attack through the Word.

Frederick Douglass once stated, "Power concedes nothing but power." What he is saying is that the lesser force will give in only to the greater force. If Satan is trying to keep you from having what God wants you to have, then to overcome you must have greater power than he does. And, according to 1 John 4:4, you have more power, because the greater Power lives in you. The Christian who is able to expend the most energy is the one who will experience victory. And, that victory will be based on our aptitude for applying Christian principles in our battle against Satan.

The same essence of victory, which is found in our capacity for change, is reflected in maximizing our potential. If you are to do extremely well in our society, you will have to maximize your gifts and talents. It is fine to have potential, but you also must know how to transform that potential into something from which people will benefit. And, to make the most of your potential, you need a force within you that is stronger than the force that is operating outside of you.

For the battlements against you to are strong and well designed. And, history will attest to the fact that even when you withstand these outside forces, they will not go away. Instead of becoming weaker, the forces that attack you in spiritual warfare actually become stronger the more you fight them. That is why it appears that you are always fighting someone. We have all experienced those times when it seemed that every issue we encountered was accompanied by another one. Stressful situations are here, and they are here to stay.

What is the source of these difficulties? The same as it has always been: Satan. And, Satan exerts a tremendous influence on people's minds. He intends to cause us to lose our footing as people of God. He does not want us to be the people that God would have us to be, or to achieve in the area in which we have been blessed with potential. But, why are we having so many difficulties battling Satan? And, why are we constantly going through trials?

One of the reasons why we find ourselves in similar situations time and time again is because we are trying to battle Satan alone. There is no victory against Satan except through the power of God. And, while we have created counter-intelligence against his attacks on our lives, we are not sufficient in ourselves. We have to allow God, who has already defeated Satan, to deal with him. There is no point in letting Satan fully beat you before turning the situation over to God. It is best to release that situation to God immediately, because He is the one most equipped to handle Satan. We know from Ephesians 6:12 that since battles are not fought in the physical realm, we must rely on God for the victory: "For we wrestle not against flesh and blood, but against principalities, against powers, against the rulers of the darkness of this world, against spiritual wickedness in high places."

You simply cannot exchange blows with Satan using the same tools that he uses. He knows more about his weapons than you do. He knows how to use them effectively, whereas you are inexperienced in their proper use. Spiritual warfare is Satan's specialty, his area of expertise. You cannot stir up trouble and tell lies the way he can. Who else can create such aggressive diseases and vicious addictions? Who else could convince you to worry over a trifle and lose sleep, when everything else is all right? He employs tactics that you never heard. And, since the battle takes place in your mind and spirit, you have to have a force within that is stronger than Satan to combat him. The only power stronger than Satan is God: so His Spirit must be integrated into yours.

First, we have to recognize that our power lies in God, and that because we have access to that power, we have the authority to effect change. That ability comes form the Spirit rather than by man's understanding or might or power. This ability to invoke change by the Spirit was an integral part of Zerubbabel's life. Zerubbabel was interested in rebuilding the city and bringing the people of God back to prominence. He desired to fortify the city so that all people would recognize God's hand was upon it.

Zerubbabel's city was in ruins, and there were various responses to this unfortunate state of affairs. Some who saw the city's condition were not concerned about it. This apathy has allowed the downfall of many Christians. Some people who profess Christ see you struggling in some area of your life and do not attempt to assist you. They simply do not respond. If we are the children of God, we are brothers and sisters in spirit. We must not exhibit indifference to a brother's decline into alcohol, a sister's into drugs or a sibling's into fornication. Yet, some people in the body of Christ still resemble the apathetic observers of Zerubbabel in their response to a Christian on the verge of ruin.

Then, there were those who had seen the city but did not want Zerubbabel to restore it. This attitude can still be seen today. Do you know that there are some people who do not want your life restored? They are interested in your always being down, in poverty, with your home split asunder. They may even move from being an observer to being an active participant in ensuring that those negative conditions do not change. They desire for you to live in misery so you can be pitiful, inviting others to join your pity party.

The people did not want Zerubbabel to restore the city, and this overwhelming response caused him some concern. So, God sent a word to him in Zechariah 4:6: "This is the word of the LORD unto Zerubbabel, saying, 'Not by might, nor by power, but by My Spirit,' saith the LORD of hosts." God was revealing to him that he would face the forces that warred against him, but not by might. There would be no physical army to protect him during his efforts. No, the force that would allow Zerubbabel to move forth would not be might. While the might of the world might come against Zerubbabel for rebuilding the city, his ability to overcome would not result from the same might.

The promises that God has given to individuals and to the church are not determined by might. There are churches with thousands of members, and if God evaluated only on the basis of their might, many of the smaller churches would not be recognized. But, God is not concerned with which churches exhibit the greatest power in terms of numbers and giving. He does not need all that to have His will fulfilled.

Peter is a profound example of how God can move without human might. When Peter received the Holy Ghost, he just stood up and declared the testimony that saved more than 3,000 souls at one time. God chose to work through one person, which illustrates essentially what He was telling Zerubbabel. He was saying that His power was sufficient unto itself, and no display of human might would be able to equal it.

It is vital that we learn that the source of our power lies in our relationship with God. It is in knowing the source of our power that we can redirect it to maximize our potential. God must be the originator of our power. He must be what influences our lives. And, if we are to maximize our potential in any area of our lives, it will be through the Spirit of God.

Our human insufficiency dictates our need for God. We need Him to assist us in changing certain areas of our lives. Because we are limited, we need His Spirit to dwell within us. If any real change is to occur in your life, God must do it. You need the baptism of the Holy Ghost so that the Spirit of God indwells you. Conversion is not enough. Shaking the pastor's hand on Sunday is not enough. Going to new member's class is not enough. You need the power of God in your life so you can withstand the insidious wiles of Satan (Ephesians 6:11). It is only through God that we have the ability to alter our circumstances, modify our personalities and behavior, and invite new opportunities into our lives.

When we allow God's Spirit to have His way in our lives, there is a greater chance that change can occur. The Word says you become a new creature in Christ (2 Corinthians 5:17), and that implies change. It is inevitable when you come to Christ. Reflect on the areas of your persona and life that have been transformed since you came to Christ. Do you handle difficult situations in the same manner as when you were in the world? Are your speech, your dress, even your interests the same? If you cannot honestly point to any changes in your life since coming to Christ, ask yourself: did I truly come to Him?

It is usually those individuals who are most in need of change who resist it the most. Since God has given you the opportunity to change yourself or to be influenced to change through someone else, it is likely that He desires change for you. Yet, it seems that people who are especially in need of change have the most excuses why they cannot change. They can tell all kinds of stories about how they changed in the past although there is little evidence to prove it. And, yet, you know that you need to get yourself together. You cannot go against God's will for you and find yourself faring well (see Jonah 1). God will not allow that to happen. And, you cannot afford to wait because you do not know the time of Jesus' return and you want to have your house in order (Luke 12:40).

Perhaps, one of the reasons you are resisting change in the spirit is because Christ is not really your God. Oh, you attend church services regularly, and you may even be a leader in one of the church departments. But, the Lord is not your God, because you worship other things. This does not refer to worshipping an idol in an obvious way, because you do not see yourself in that light. But, when you emphasize maintaining your big house and luxury import car more than reading the Word and praying, then whom do you serve? If the hours you work to preserve a certain lifestyle affect your ability to make it to church services and fellowship, what are your priorities? You are concerned with everything but God.

We must be receptive and sensitive to the moving of God in our lives, and this is possible through His Word. One of the paradoxes of the Christian life is that if we are grounded in His Word, we are given the ability to soar to great heights in the spirit and in society. The explosiveness of the Word makes people who have the ability to do great things. You can maximize your abilities to such an extent that it inspires change in other people's lives. You can maximize your talents to the point where it is now profitable for you. You can maximize your potential so that you are utilizing a skill instead or just talking about it. You can do it!

Once you have exhibited a true desire for change, you must allow its transforming power to be released. It is not enough to just desire change; you have to open yourself up to allow change to take place. We cannot modify anything in our lives until we become more honest and open with God. What do you want Him to do for you? Be specific about the areas in which you desire God to mobilize your spirit to change.

After calling on the Spirit in regard to our needs, it is our spiritual responsibility to actually foster that change ourselves. We are going through God, because the power we have is His. But, we are the ones who must actually make the effort required for any degree of change. There are no magicians who will instantly fulfill your desire. And, while God has given you power, you have to work in the spirit and in the physical realm.

Our sufficiency is in God, so whatever we are to be is through Him. After appropriating His power, there still must be a desire on your part that something be done. The Word says, "Delight thyself also in the LORD; and he shall give thee the desires of thine heart" (Psalm 37:4). You will not have anything come to you until you express your desires.

What is it that you want? Do you want to be a stronger Christian, so that your light is a representation of God to man? Do you want the Holy Ghost? Do you want to be empowered to maximize your potential, to do more than you ever imagined? Or, do you want the anointing of God in your life? You are saying to God, "I desire the spiritual fortitude and stamina so I can stand up and be counted on, and also be counted for." If you desire that change so you can be the person He wants you to be, move out in authority on it. We have got to get our spirit right, and then other things will change for us as well.

The message that the Lord revealed to Zerubbabel is applicable for us today. We are not to depend on tangible presentations of might and power, because those things will ultimately fail us. Our trust is to remain in God, who has equipped us through His Spirit. The Spirit has empowered us to change those facets of our lives that need changing and to maximize our gifts to a higher plane. But, more importantly, He has granted us to recognize that our battles, and yes, even our victories belong not to us, but to the Lord.

Chapter Five

Using What You Have

"The dichotomy of your possessing potential is that it belongs to God."

When you accept the premise that you can change your life through Christ, the first thing that assaults this belief is the spirit of doubt. Doubt, by its insidious nature, begins to corrode the developing faith that some real change is about to occur in your life. It is that incessant voice that projects all your insecurities and fears to the forefront of your consciousness. And, it has the very real power to affect your perspective on a situation. This is because doubt undermines any hope or belief.

You have tried living outside the will of God, and have painfully learned that this path does not carry you to the level to which you aspire. So, you finally surrender to God's call on your life in hopes that submission will guard you from the harsher aspects of life. You have come to understand that through Christ, you can change your life, vivify your persona, release the burdens of your past and fulfill your dreams.

And, whether we mobilize ourselves to act on it or not, we all carry with us a picture of who we can be. Although that picture may bear little resemblance to who we are now, God says that we have become new creatures in Him (2 Corinthians 5:17), and thus have the opportunity and ability to evolve into that image. Initially, with the fury of possibilities, you fully believe this. But, you were not prepared to have periods of doubt. It seems the dream is still out of reach. You are going through more now than you did when you were in the world, and His voice is yet silent on the direction your life should take. You joined the church Sunday morning and are dismayed when He does not answer you in time for the evening news. God is not as interested in members as He is in believers. And, because you have not grown to maturity as a Christian, you allow doubt to permeate your spirit.

The most insidious and demoralizing effect of doubt is that it puts you in bondage. This simply means that you are now fearful of seeing change, and experience some reservations in regard to God's presence in your life. This is the state in which Satan wants you to remain. He can eventually move you closer to the ways of the world, which he orchestrates, if you are not sure what you believe about the validity of God's promises.

How do we know that Satan is responsible for our state of bondage? We know from the Word that the character of God exemplifies the attributes of liberty: "...where the Spirit of the Lord is, there is liberty" (2 Corinthian 3:17b). Thus, God does not relegate us to bondage, because bondage is contrary to His nature. Romans 8:15 states, "For ye have not received the spirit of bondage again to fear; but ye have received the Spirit of adoption" — that is, sonship.

If you have ever sensed the presence of bondage or are in bondage now, it is time to free yourself from those shackles, because they are not of God.

The Scripture does not state that you do not have an attitude of bondage or that you are not bound in the flesh. But, it does say that you have not received the spirit of bondage again to fear. That means that the Spirit of God indwells you, which makes all things concerning you positive. This is because the Spirit of God is one of liberty and emancipation.

Why do we say "emancipation"? Because, if you were bound prior to receiving the Spirit, you become free once He indwells you. And, the Spirit that God gives you does not cause you to backslide into the lifestyle and habits practiced of the past. If you were in fear prior to receiving the Spirit, He changes that, because you now partake of the very nature of God. Remember, God did not give you a spirit of fear (2 Timothy 1:7). Furthermore, the nature of God is not one of fear.

How do we know that we do not have the spirit of bondage that comes from Satan? We know because we have been adopted as children of God, and He is our Father. There cannot be opposing spirits indwelling us. There is no dichotomy either in the Spirit of God or in our relationship with Him; we are one and the same. John 17:20-21a says, "Neither pray I for these alone, but for them also which shall believe on Me through their word;

That they all may be one; as Thou, Father, art in Me, and I in Thee...." We are able to resist this spirit of bondage once we understand that it is not of God. And, if God's Spirit is within us, then that other restricting spirit has no part in us

We have to restructure our thinking in terms of points of identification. Our focus must be on identifying with the Spirit more than with the flesh. But, the reality is that many Christians still take their identity from who they are in the flesh. Romans 8:5 states, "For they that are after the flesh do mind the things of the flesh; but they that are after the Spirit the things of the Spirit." The hindrances, the immobility and the inhibitions that you experience are things that exist in the flesh. And, it is the flesh that limits your ability to achieve.

As long as you identify with the flesh, you will always see the obstacles before the finished product. You will always be confronted with why you cannot fulfill your dream. The vision will stay clouded. The impossible remains just that when you operate out of the flesh. This is because the flesh can only deal with material things. It cannot comprehend the moving of God in your life. In Matthew 17:27, Jesus commanded Peter to suspend his identification with material things and move in the Spirit. Jesus tells him to "...go thou to the sea, and cast an hook, take up the fish that first cometh up; and when thou hast opened his mouth, thou shalt find a piece of money." Peter knew that fish did not have a diet of money, so he could have been paralyzed by the improbability of what Jesus was saying to him. But, because he chose not to listen to the dictates of the flesh, Peter was able to receive the miracle of what Jesus said would be there.

The flesh keeps us from achieving at the level God wants for us. We have a God who has prepared us to go beyond thoughts of the flesh; He is powerful and can handle all matters, whether in the flesh or in the spirit. When Christ comes into your life, you do not simply exist; you live! He brings life to the life He had on earth. But, what happens is that we have a tendency, after having received God, to go back to satisfying the flesh. Those who are in the Spirit want to know where God is taking them. But, how can you ask God when you are preoccupied with worldly issues? You cannot speak to God because you are hurt that someone did not speak to you; you are hurting because someone else got that promotion; you are hurting because of past situations and misunderstandings. It is time to come out of that old mindset into newness of life so that you can identify with where God wants you today.

Our reality should not be living in the present with the pain of the past. If we are carnally minded, meaning we allow ourselves to be led by the flesh, then there is no life in us. Romans 8:6 says, "For to be carnally minded is death; but to be spiritually minded is life and peace." The focus here is not physical death, but lifelessness in terms of attitude toward and enthusiasm for Christ. The reference is to spiritual death as it relates to identifying with the Spirit of God. Being carnally minded ensures that we will be unable to see things differently than the world or to have insight into the ways of God. The Bible declares in 1 Corinthians 2:14 that "...the natural man receiveth not the things of the Spirit of God... because they are spiritually discerned." God is moving in one direction, and you are oblivious because you are spiritually dead.

Many professing Christians have lost their spiritual footing because they did not understand what God was trying to do in their lives. You cannot understand God through your intellect. Your knowledge of Him is obtained in the Spirit and can only be enhanced by careful study of His Word. The intellect is an element of the carnality of man. Your emphasis on things of this world will alienate you from the blessings that occur in the Spirit. God is consistent, and He will move in your life if you embark on the things that He has already given you. If you can be faithful on this level, God will move you into an increasing awareness of Him and into a place you have not been before. Then, when the Spirit energizes you, you can go and tell someone else about God and what He did for you.

There is life and peace in being spiritually minded. When you are uninhibited by the flesh, when you are not limited in your spirit, you know in your mind that you are able to achieve without being hindered by anything or anyone. When you are focused on living in the Spirit, you are walking around charged up and on fire, saying, "Lord, what else do you want me to do?" Going to church is not something that you do out of tradition or obligation, but because you are enthused about worshipping God. You should be involved in the ministry because of enthusiasm. You are a witness to the favor of God at your job, in your home, even on the street because you cannot help but share how good He has been to you. Whatever it takes to walk in God's will is spiritual living.

We can experience spiritual living by saturating our minds with the Word of God. This saturation with the Word of God sets you at liberty. This is the spiritual condition that God desires for you, and it is a positive one. If we are living in fear, we cannot maximize our potential because we will be afraid of doing anything out of the ordinary. But, because the Spirit of God gives freedom and liberty (2 Corinthians 3:17b), we can achieve at the level God desires for us.

Has there ever been a time in your life when you had an abundance of financial resources? Perhaps, you previously could only meet the bills, but now you have a little extra to enjoy yourself. Think about how you enjoyed the freedom of shopping. Does it not feel good to be able to meet a payment when it is due and not feel bound when that due date approached? Your behavior changes when you are not bound by the need to economize. The restriction is taken away. Similarly, in Christ, the restrictions have been removed, and this is the time to enjoy spiritual living. This is the time for explosiveness, for choice and for maximizing your potential without being mired in mediocrity.

With the restrictions removed, we are free to express ourselves in the Lord. We have the freedom to maximize our gifts so that they prove beneficial for others. We are free to witness about the presence of God and to give evidence of His presence through our testimony. We are free to enjoy opportunities, knowing that God has orchestrated them for our renewal and advancement. There is freedom to bring to fruition those things that you know the Lord has promised you.

You have to come to understand who you are in Christ. No one can determine that for you. You are a child of God and you need to know you have access to His power. "For the law of the Spirit of life in Christ Jesus hath made me free from the law of sin and death" (Romans 8:2). Just as the children of Israel were given the Ten Commandments to bring them into an awareness of how to live, so you also have been exposed to the knowledge of what Christians are expected to do. God lets you know that He is the only One and that you are to serve Him. Yet, we struggle with putting this simple concept into practice. We need only look at the world and see how His children serve the idols of beauty, money, sex, power and other temporary fulfillments to know that this fundamental concept is continually violated.

But, thank God for the law of life in the Spirit! When you experience spiritual living, you know you do not need another god, because you have learned through the Spirit that He is the only true and living God. You have been blessed greatly, and you know that He has been so good to you that you cannot even conceptualize another god in His stead. When you know God, you become so in love with Him that there is nothing that you will not do for Him. Operating in the law of life through the Spirit makes a real difference in your life. This is because it takes you from a state of bondage to wonderful freedom.

This new freedom will cause you to love God to the point that you are willing to do whatever He wants. "I'll go out and reach the lost because I love You. I'll help the downtrodden because I love You. I'll help build your church because I love You." If you love God in the manner that you should, if you are spiritually minded and not carnally minded, you will know there is not anyone anywhere who loves you more than God does. Your love for others can never equal God's love for you, and yet that is precisely what He desires from you. When you show love for God, He will move the mountains in your life. He will crack open the previously closed door so that we can enter into what was denied to you. He will take the little you have and maximize it so that you can receive more than what you expected to have.

Our identification with the Spirit of God allows us to maximize our potential because whatever God has, we have. If He operates from liberty, then so should we. If you know that God has ordained you, then you have the credibility to move ahead. Since you know that God has ordered your steps, walk in those steps. If He has shown you the path for your life, then move in that direction, looking neither to the left nor to the right. Since He has equipped you with certain abilities, utilize the abilities that you have. Our abstention from the flesh is what allows us to walk in the Spirit. And, God reveals to us what we have and whom we are when we take up residence in the Spirit.

When you know who you are and where you are, you have to disassociate from carnal influences. Be prepared to say to yourself, "God has ordained me for this time and I have to move into His promises for my life." The reason you must separate yourself from those who are carnally minded is that they offer insidious reminders of failed attempts in your past. They reveal to you what you are, but only in terms of your worldly image. They have no power over your life in the Spirit if you recognize that God accepts you with all your deficiencies. You have not received the spirit of bondage, and it cannot overcome you. You can move beyond carnality and fear because you have the Spirit of God in you.

The Spirit of God is an intimate part of you. We have to stop viewing God as an abstract being in the sky and start seeing Him as a familiar Person Who indwells us. He is our Father, and that denotes that we are His children. The Spirit Himself bears witness that we are His children. And, for that level of kinship to be established, there must be a relationship between the parties. When you can accept God as your Father in a real sense, then your perception about yourself will change. You will not allow the same types of people to be a part of your intimate circle. You will not place yourself in the same situations as you did before. You cannot help but have changes in your attitude and behavior when you really understand who you are in Him.

The Spirit tells you to use what you have. He says you can do it! You can go through difficulties and remain whole. He wants you to accept the difficulties in your life and use them for your good. It is not manifested in the flesh, but in the Spirit. In the Spirit we already have what we want; it just has not manifested itself in the flesh (2 Peter 1:3). You may not yet see it, but you already have what you need.

You do not understand how you can achieve something, but you can start with what you have, because you are operating in the Spirit. Change has not yet occurred in into your life, but in the Spirit you can see the change. You are still in pain, but in the Spirit you can see healing. Peace has not yet entered your home, but through the Spirit you can speak peace. You are currently in debt, but in the Spirit you can see release. You are unemployed now, but in the Spirit you can envision working.

However, you must abstain from gratifying the flesh and move into the Spirit. You have to program yourself to satisfy the Spirit. That is, you must live in a manner that is consistent with being an heir of God. Although you have not seen God, you have seen evidence of Him. This evidence tells you that the earth is His and the fullness thereof, the world and all that dwell there; that the cattle on a thousand hills belong to Him; that the earth is His footstool and the heavens His dwelling place. You have not seen Him, but you know that His ears still hear you and His arms yet save. The evidence tells you that He was the One who created everything: scooped out the seas, hung the stars in space, fastened the moon against the sky and molded the mountains.

Although you have not seen God, the evidence tells you He is and that you are an heir (Romans 8:17). Scripture tells us that God so loved the world that He gave His only begotten son (John 3:16a). So, if you are an heir of God with His only begotten Son, then what do you expect to receive from Him? We know what God did for His Son: He set Him on His right hand when He returned to glory. And, as an heir, you should expect to receive all the benefits Jesus received in the Spirit. You occupy the same place that Jesus does as a joint heir. How do you know that? In the Spirit!

If we are heirs with Christ, then why do we still experience pain and suffering? For one thing, Jesus endured similar experiences, and we should not expect to endure less than He did. But, you can get out of these experiences if you desire. When you become tired of going through a difficulty, you will get out of it. When you have taken enough pressure, you will get out of it. It is just a matter of releasing your burdens and proclaiming, "No more!" God has given us the Spirit so that we can be liberated in Him. So, take the little that you have and maximize it. Do all you can with what God has given you. Take what little joy you have and increase it. Maximize your reservoir of peace, of knowledge, of love. Take whatever you have and use it to the greatest possible extent so that you can be content in the knowledge that you have maximized what you have.

Chapter Six

Trusting in God

"The effects of trust are both a release and a relief."

In accepting that we can maximize what we presently have for Christ, we must also trust that Christ has already secured that ability within us. We have all experienced the fear that we will lose something of value. This may refer to possession, loved ones, earned positions, accumulated wealth, etc.... Whatever embodies that fear for you, there has been a time in your life when it appeared that what was rightfully yours might be taken away. You had worked hard to achieve a certain position, and just as they were about to bestow that new title on you, someone or something came along to try to take it away. Or, you did and said all the right things to garner that special someone's attention, and when he or she seemed within your grasp, someone jeopardized that opportunity for you.

The circumstances are as varied as the individuals, but what binds us to others is that we have all been placed in a fearful situation — fearful in the sense that we were challenged by that situation, experienced levels of apprehension about the results, or felt ourselves on the verge of losing something. It does not matter who you are or what position you occupy in life, someone or something has purposely tried to hinder you from having what you perceived as yours. And, the effect of that interaction is most often fear.

While we know that these experiences will happen, it is of greater importance that you know what to do in these situations. You have to know where to turn for guidance. You need to know the source of true strength. You need to understand why you are under attack in the first place. If you do not know what the enemy seeks from you, you will not know what to protect or how to protect it.

So, what do you do? The most important thing is to trust in God's plan for your life. While most Christians are familiar with the concept of trusting in the Lord, how do we translate this notion into a working reality? There must first be transference from nodding the head in church to an authentic working out of this belief in the crucible of our lives. It is not enough for us to simply have a belief; we must apply that belief to release its empowering properties.

2 Chronicles 20:1 offers a deeper understanding of this concept. It tells the story of victory as a result of King Jehoshaphat trusting in the Lord. We know that a great number of enemies were coming against this king, and that he was fearful, just as we have been apprehensive when we have found ourselves in difficult situations that threatened our sense of stability. Jehoshaphat had armies coming against him, and while our enemies may come in different forms, it is their coming that elicits the initial response of fear.

The emphasis on the idea of the enemy coming highlights the perceived sense of a greater power advancing on one's own lesser power. The fact that someone is coming against you indicates that they at least believe they can annihilate you. And, if you are unprepared for an enemy, it is probable that you have little defense against an attack. Satan knows which Christians are prepared to battle him, because they already have on their armor and are living as soldiers for the Gospel. He already knows that power is God's power and that it can subdue him. So, he looks for the church member who is defenseless, who has not been praying, fasting and reading the Word. Remember, he is "seeking whom he may devour" (1 Peter 5:8b). And, Satan attacks those who do not have a relationship with Christ because he knows their power is only their own.

So, when the enemy descends on you, it is an alarming experience. It is important to look at this fear as because it has an alienating effect on those who are experiencing it. And, by definition, alienation involves separation from the place we formerly occupied and the people with whom we shared attachments. The most detrimental effect of alienation is that it often removes us from God's covering and creates distance in our personal relationship with Him. And, the progression from fear to alienation decidedly affects our ability to trust the Lord.

So, we find that Jehoshaphat's first response to the news of his enemies coming was not one of trust. He did not receive the news in a spirit of contentment, knowing God would protect him. He did not smile and wave the messenger away in good humor at the idea of being attacked. No, he was afraid. Yet, the Bible does not suggest that he was a terrible believer to have allowed this news to initially affect him this way.

It is normal to experience dismay in the presence of danger; and strength often comes out of the very situations that elicit it. While the Lord has not given us a spirit of fear, our flesh does have a tendency to respond with some degree of trepidation. However minute, we have all heard something frightening or damaging and thought to ourselves, "Oh, my God, what am I going to do?"

We have to recognize that hindering forces can produce alarm, even through it is not of God's Spirit. Our flesh still responds to earthly stimuli, and only as we learn to trust the Lord does that tendency decrease. Yet, those situations that inspire trepidation can also offer the redeeming opportunity to grow in strength. Such was the case for Jehoshaphat, in that, after he feared, he turned to the Lord. And, regardless of our initial response, God wants us to trust and turn to Him in difficult times.

Christians often experience fear before exercising a degree of trust in the Lord. Yet, it is fear that will cause you to go in either a negative or positive direction. To Jehoshaphat's credit he did not flee, and he turned immediately to the Lord. Many times we exacerbate the problem by running from it instead of asking the Lord to help us deal with it. Jehoshaphat dealt with his problem by instructing all of Judah to fast, because he understood that if he was captured, then so was all of Judah.

But, what relation has a Biblical king to the pressing concerns of your contemporary life? Oh, it is a great story for learning to trust, but you do not see the coming of armies as relevant to your life. The Moabites and Ammonites do not cause the same level of anxiety in you as foreclosure, bankruptcy, and divorce. What are armies to you when there are bill collectors threatening your security, loved ones shaking your faith, and sickness robbing you of your mobility?

You have to understand when you are going through a crisis that the battle is not just against you. You must focus on the fact that the body of Christ consists of many members (1 Corinthians 12:12, 14). You are just one of the members. The battle in which you find yourself is against every believer in the Lord. So, whenever the devil attacks you, your marriage, your home, you children, your job, he is really attacking the kingdom of God. You just happen to be in the way. Perhaps, you think Satan is after you because you are so important, but he is not thinking about your name. He is not concerned about your title or position. Satan is concerned only about tearing down God's kingdom.

There is one essential point of connection for us to Jehoshaphat's experience. Jehoshaphat understood that the armies were coming not only against him, but also against all the people in his land. And, the enemy knew that conquering the king was tantamount to conquering all the people of Judah. In the same way, Satan sees destroying you as symbolic of destroying all believers in God.

Satan knows that if he can get you, then you can provide greater access to your friends. Then, when he has your friends, he has access to a network of people whom he can cause to react negatively and to stop praying and praising God. Satan knows that the more Christian lives he damages, the more workers he lays off from the task of kingdom building.

In reflecting on how you handle fear, the greater issue arises of how you can move from being afraid to trusting God for deliverance. How do you lean on a Spirit when we have been conditioned to trust in the physical (and even that disappoints)? How do you trust when you are not even sure how to trust? Oh, you know what Webster's says, but in the midst of trials, that does not offer much help.

Jehoshaphat found himself in the same position as many of us today. He understood that moving from fear to trust required several things of him. He knew that trust consisted of allowing God to handle his concerns. In a more practical sense, he went to God and asked Him for assistance and direction. Next, he believed that God would respond to his needs. Then, he actually waited on the Lord to move on his behalf.

But, Jehoshaphat understood what many Christians today do not: you must put yourself in a position to hear God. And, the most powerful and effective way to do this is to fast. The king called for a nationwide fast in Judah, and God responded by defending them against their enemies. This is because fasting is the most direct exercise you can undertake to move God. If there was ever a way to accomplish whatever you want; it is through fasting. God sees this as an outward indication of an inner sincerity, a demonstration of your trust in Him.

Fasting also expresses the urgency you feel concerning a situation in your life. When difficult circumstances arise, fasting says, "God, I need immediate attention." While it does not take away the pressure of those circumstances, it does bring you to the place of submission. God wants us to ask for help and to give all our troubles to Him. Remember that your troubles are not really about you, but are aimed directly at God for the purpose of destroying His kingdom. And, since we Christians are a part of His kingdom, Satan targets us. The way to move beyond your troubles is to communicate your need through fasting. And, it is through the submission of fasting that we are most open to hearing what God is saying.

While individual fasting brings one closer to deliverance, it is through group participation that the greatest power of fasting is released. Notice that the king did not fast alone in his chambers. 2 Chronicles 20:4 states, "And Judah gathered themselves together, to ask help of the Lord: even out of all the cities of Judah they came to seek the Lord." Jehoshaphat called an entire country to fast;

he understood that the intensity of the group inspires a greater response than does one man alone. Fasting together brought them together with a common goal and a common place to take action.

We must learn to fast, not only alone, but also together as we seek after God. Someone may say, "Well, she's not going through the same problem I am, so how can we fast together?" But, fasting together gives clarity in the areas of concern for all involved. God can speak to each of us individually, even in a group. But, the strength resides in the unity and in the shared goal of being delivered by God. When there is a concerted effort, you bring corporate anointing into your midst. And, the more you implement fasting into your spiritual walk, the greater your urgency to move forward in the manner in which every Christian should. You will not even wait for the pastor to proclaim a fast because you will sense the need for it in your own spirit. And, you will begin encouraging other Christians to fast as well. You will find yourself, for the first time, in the unique position of really understanding the direction in which Christ wants you to move.

Perhaps, you remain unconvinced of the validity of fasting for deliverance. Perhaps, you exist in a sphere where problems are concepts to be analytically broken down and given temporary solutions. But, those with the vision to see the Ammonites yet advancing on us in contemporary array understand that fasting is critical. The Ammonites are still gathering against the body of Christ! Only this time they are stealthily encroaching upon us in the camouflages of drugs, violence, gangs and disruptions in the homes and schools.

The partner and enhancer of fasting is prayer. Prayer is comprised not only of expressing your needs and thanks to the Lord, but also of keeping yourself before Him. The importance of the latter is further expressed in 2 Chronicles 20:5. "And Jehoshaphat stood in the congregation of Judah and Jerusalem, in the house of the Lord, before the new court." It is important to note that he positioned himself close to God.

Unfortunately, when we are confronted with like situations, we do not always put ourselves in proximity to the power we need. People will find themselves in certain situations, and their first response is to keep to themselves and stay out of church. The worst place to be in the midst of trouble is alone. First, you deny God the freedom to move in your life because you have isolated yourself, and then, you alienate other Christians who can aid you in your battles through communal fasts and prayer.

The value of focusing on the experience of Jehoshaphat is that it offers timeless revelations about human response and the power of trusting in the Lord. As revealed through the king's situation, prayer recognizes God as the source of life and all things. If you can acknowledge God as the Creator of everything, it becomes less difficult to trust Him to handle some portions of the world that He made. In 2 Chronicles 20:6, Jehoshaphat prays, "O Lord God of our fathers, art not Thou God in heaven? And rulest not Thou over all the kingdoms of the heathen? And in Thine hand is there not power and might, so that none is able to withstand Thee?"

Since He is that same God today, does He not still retain the ability to provide and protect during the troubling times in your life? He has never relinquished His power and might, and if He is with you and you in Him, you can subdue your enemy. When you understand the mobilizing power of prayer, your relationship with Christ deepens and your life is renewed. Your relationship becomes more profound because He knows you through your prayers. And, you are learning more about Christ through communicating with Him.

If you want to get God immediately involved in your situation, you need to show Him through humility of spirit that you cannot do it alone. If your attitude is, "Look, God, I don't need You because I can figure out a way to do it," where do you leave room for Him to enter into your life? The reality is that you do need Him to move on your behalf. The only reason why Jehoshaphat was successful in dealing with his enemies was because God allowed him to be. God told him to march down and meet the enemy, knowing they did not have sufficient military power. But, if God does not tell you to go against the multitude, you had better keep still. Sometimes, we make decisions without consulting Him and are surprised to find ourselves in a fix.

It is important that we continue learning how to pray, because the Spirit will move someone during communal prayer just as with solitary prayer. In 2 Chronicles 20:15, the Spirit informs Jahaziel through prayer what to say to Jehoshaphat: "Hearken ye, all Judah, and ye inhabitants of Jerusalem, and thou king Jehoshaphat, thus saith the Lord unto you, 'Be not afraid nor dismayed by reason of this great multitude; for the battle is not yours, but God's.'" The response was that they fasted and then prayed together, which still an effective example to imitate. This is because their communal fast brought disparate persons into oneness and humility and their collective prayer brought results from God. If "the effectual fervent prayer of a righteous man availeth much" (James 5:16b), how much more then does the shared prayer of an entire nation?

It is also essential that we pray specifically so that God knows the areas that we need Him to handle. When we pray, we move God. When we pray, we stir heaven. When we pray, we invite Him into our midst. And, when God comes, it is with positive results and for your good. It is prayer that brings the anointing into your life and alters it. And, specific prayer assures us of God's response in a specific area. If we pray too generally, we may not even recognize the areas in our lives that need strengthening. But, do not think when God answers your prayer, it is the answer that you would prefer. Often, the first thing that God directs you to do is the thing you least wanted to do. Do you think that Jehoshaphat wanted to meet the vast enemy with his meager army? It required that he trust the Lord.

Whatever you are going through, do not believe that God is going to allow you to bypass that situation. It is more likely that He is going to send you right into the midst of it. Shadrach, Meshach, and Abednego had to go right into the fire (Daniel 3). But, had they not gone into the fire, they would not have been delivered from the fire. Most of us want to be outside the fire, holding an extinguisher, shouting about how God delivered us. But, the greater testimony is from those who were in the fire, because they know that when they are going through a difficult situation, God will help them in that situation.

Learn not to run from your battles in life, because the Lord does not intend for you to fight them. He just needs you to trust Him to handle them for you. You will not need to fight, but He wants you to have the confidence to face your enemy knowing you no longer need to hide. And, as you engage in fasting and praying, it will strengthen your belief in what God will do for you. Through these practices you will develop a greater relationship with God and position yourself to receive more intimate communications from Him.

Furthermore, in all our communications with God, we must pray expectantly. We need to be confident that Christ will handle whatever issue we present to Him. This is an act of trusting and believing that change has already taken place in the spiritual realm, and it is only waiting to be manifested in the physical realm. Yet, that level of trust is required of Christians. After all, Christ has given us everything we need for spiritual living, and trusts us to do what we say. How many promises have you made to God on the condition that He would honor that one burning request? How often were you consistent with your word and promises? The beauty of knowing Christ lies in the fact that He never fails.

When God honors our prayers by answering them, it is imperative that we show our appreciation through praise. We rush to show gratitude to people who may or may not be as unfailing the next time we need them. But, to Him who is always available to us, who has never turned away from us no matter how badly we have behaved, who has supplied all our needs: to Him we are slow in giving thanks, if we do at all.

Praise is most effective when preceded by prayer and fasting. This is because fasting has already expressed your sincerity in coming to God with your needs. It has also taught you how to hear God so that you can distinguish between what He wants for you and what you desire. So, fasting becomes an opportunity to develop trust because you believe God sees you and will honor your coming to Him. This is critical because many people tell God their needs but do not wait for divine direction. This is simply going through the motions. "Well, I asked God what to do and it seemed to match what I had thought anyway." No, it did not. You had already decided what you were going to do, and simply engaged in the activity of fasting so you could justify your plan.

In like manner, your prayer must be grounded in trust for several reasons. One is that if you trust God to move on your behalf, you can have assurance in your spirit. You already know He is going to do whatever He said He would do for you. So, you do not have to run around crying with little boxes of tissues anymore. When you express this newfound trust, you will discover that those things that used to keep you from sleeping and eating no longer affect you. You can now approach situations with confidence, knowing that God can and will handle them for you.

The other reason it is essential that you trust God in prayer is so that you will not try to solve the problem or fight the battle yourself. This is really important. What is the point of presenting a problem before God if you are going to handle it in you own limited manner? In so doing, we increasingly make matters worse. He has already told you in His Word that the battle is not yours. So, why assume responsibility for what God is accountable for?

Once you have developed your ability to fast and pray, praise is the result. Praise is simply giving honor and thanks to God for all He has done for you and all that He is. It is not to be given only when your needs are answered and life is good. The challenge is to praise God when you are going through tough times. This is how He knows that you really trust Him. It is when you can praise Him when you least see Him moving in your life that you experience the greatest blessings.

Praise is the highest expression of gratitude, worship and respect. When you are going through difficulties and receive a defining word from God, give Him praise. Praise is both an inward and outward expression of love. It can be done silently, or by raising your voice in loud song and thanksgiving. There is not a standard way to praise God, only the mandate that we do so.

Praising God is also one of the ways to ensure your enemies' defeat. 2 Chronicles 20:22 says, "And when they began to sing and to praise, the Lord set ambushments against the children of Ammon, Moab, and mount Seir, which were come against Judah; and they were smitten." Because the country praised God in advance, their expectation of victory was fulfilled. God destroyed all their enemies without their ever having to get involved. How much turmoil and stress we would save ourselves if we believed every time that God would fight our battles.

But, too many Christians struggle with trusting God to handle every aspect of their lives. We consult Him about our jobs, but not about our marriage partner. It is fine to confer with Him about our children's friends, but we will not present our own friends for examination. "Oh, God, You can look after my children, but I'd better figure out my finances myself." And, when a situation is overwhelming, we would rather fail trying to deal with it ourselves than give it to God in the beginning.

Do you believe that you are any less in the eyes of God than His other children? If not, then you must embrace this truth: God will do for you anything that you ask Him if you believe in Him. He is no respecter of persons; He honors not only the prayers of those in the Bible. He is not a God who uses man's limited criteria for blessing you. God has preserved these accounts in the Bible so that you might understand two things: He will exercise His power and love on behalf of His children, and if He did something for someone else, He will do the same for you whom He loves just as dearly.

The Bible further reveals the significance of praising the Lord. 2 Chronicles 20:21 says, "And when he had consulted with the people, he appointed singers unto the Lord, and that should praise the beauty of holiness, as they went out before the army, and to say, Praise the Lord; for His mercy endureth for ever." He sent a praise team into battle in front of the army. The positioning of the praise team is important because they were not going to use the same weapons as the enemy. They were not armed with spears, swords and shield but with songs of praise for the Lord.

In the face of imminent destruction, the singers praised God for His mercy and love. Why would they sing a song of praise when they were about to be attacked? Because, they had already heard from God and understood that all power, glory, dominion and honor belongs to Him. And, when they sang praises, the Lord confused the enemy and caused them to destroy each other.

We have to learn to be praise singers in our own right. This experience reveals to us the dramatic response of the Lord when we offer up our praise. Have you ever been praised for doing a good job, being a great partner, or organizing a community event? You were already going to perform the task because that was the role assigned to you. But, when you received that praise, were you not motivated to do more, to really shine in your role? Well, that is how praise works with God too. It is His role to take care of us, but praise gives Him the incentive to really shine on our behalf.

And, what can we anticipate as the results of our praise? 2 Chronicles 20:30 states, "So the realm of Jehoshaphat was quiet: for his God gave him rest round about." We can expect like rewards of relief and peace in those areas of our lives that are being attacked. If you praise Him, He can give you peace and protect you from your adversaries. He can lift you out of the valley, create a passage across the mountain, send spiritual refreshment in barren times, cast light into the darkness, God will deliver you.

In the process of growing with God, we can develop a deeper relationship of trust. It will be difficult to move into His will without it, because spiritual living requires changes that we cannot justify with our intellect. We simply have to trust the Word of God and move when and how we are directed. In this way we are positioning ourselves to more greatly maximize our potential.

As we incorporate fasting into our lives, we will discover that we can hear the Lord more clearly. And, that makes us more sensitive to what He wants us to do. By extension, this process naturally leads to prayer, which is a cornerstone of our relationship with Christ. This relationship is not unlike our worldly relationships in the sense that it must be tended in order to survive, and this maintenance transpires through prayer. The culmination of fasting and prayer is praise. Each discipline is a means of directly communicating with God, but together they represent a fundamental exercise in developing trust in God and His plan for our lives. And, trust is essentially the conduit that God uses to show us how to greater maximize our potential.

Chapter Seven

Creating Our Character

"Knowing who we are is not always synonymous with loving who we are."

Society has imbedded the idea in our consciousness that we are products of our environment and our history. Thus, we are defined by our surroundings, and family pedigrees dictate our natural limitations. Our parents were a certain caliber of people, so we are too. Our neighborhoods restricted us to low levels of exposure to culture and opportunities, so our vision is limited. Our education was designed for only a certain level of advancement, so we strain against a ceiling. This is what we have consistently been given to understand. Yet, the greatest indicator of the depth and distance of our life journey lies more in our character than in the external gauges of our progress.

For a Christian, the idea that our lives are predetermined by our history and environment is a particularly unsatisfactory foundation for growth. This is because it sets up the premise that there is no opportunity for change because everything has already been determined. And, for people coming out of the world into the bosom of Christ, change is the vehicle by which one makes that transition. So, if you accept society's philosophy of placement based on external factors, you are doing more than actively setting limitations for yourself. You are essentially giving the world permission to defeat you.

So, in light of the world's perspective, what view can we adopt for Christian living? We can choose to believe persuasive evidence that Christian living not only allows for change, but also demands it. And, where there is change, there are tremendous opportunities for growth. When you come to Christ, you become a new person through your rebirth. This rebirth is essentially your surrendering the self so that Christ can transform you into His likeness. It seems improbable that your behavior and thoughts could undergo a transformation when you come to Christ.

This is because the ways of the world are in direct opposition to Christian living. Those things that society glorifies are the very things that Christianity will move you away from. It is impossible to reconcile that the world encourages sexuality in various modes while the Bible states that fornication is a sin. This belief, like many in the Bible, forces you to be on one side of the fence or the other.

You can straddle the fence and attempt to justify following both the world and God; but yet, for whom are you performing? God sees you as you truly are, just as you do. Therefore, when we do not follow the instructions in the Bible, we are seen by the only observer who matters: God. What does it really matter if church folks believe we are saved because of our facade at the 11a.m. hour, when we stay from our teaching at midnight?

Once we understand that Christ does not base His expectations of us on our history as people do, we can begin to claim newness and change in our lives. People would have us believe that we have already established who we are and cannot move outside of those limitations. The reason why people do not encourage us to improve ourselves is that they are already comfortable with a certain perspective. It is comforting for them to think they already know all about you. In believing they know you, they are essentially saying they also know your opportunities, your chance for blessings, and your place in society.

Another reason why people (church folks included) participate in defining your limitations is that they do not want you to get ahead of them. They are fearful that if you are given encouragement, you might actually achieve your potential. We have all known people who had incredible potential to achieve, yet because of lack of confidence, did not move forward. But, what if they were given the support necessary to energize them to utilize what God had given them? Now imagine that same person using their talents and abilities. Would they have surpassed you in your present state? It is the possibility of this revised vision that has people working against your being mobilized into newness in Christ.

If Christ does not relegate us to our past (2 Corinthians 5:16-17), then we can be certain that the present is ours. We can use the present in our lives to renew ourselves and discover who God has called us to be. And, this discovery is preceded by the study of God's Word. This is because the Word is the means by which we learn about Christ. And, learning about Christ is essential to learning about ourselves. Since Christ is our model for living, it is essential that we know Him, and that is possible only through study and prayer. This process is critical because we have to learn, as we cast off the old self, whom we must become in Christ.

Why does Christ require us to become new creatures through Him? For one thing, He must reshape your thoughts and behavior so that your life will be consistent with His Word (Romans 12:2). This means that your life must now reflect obedience to His instructions for living. And, the power of His instructions is that they are designed for you to have an intimate relationship with Him, as well as a higher quality of life. It is not true that living for Christ keeps you from enjoying life, as worldly people would encourage you to believe. The change is that now, instead of following hedonistic impulses, your agenda is to please God.

Next, God has to empower you with His Word so that He can use you for good in the world. In order to be used by God, you have to know Him, and that intimacy is developed through reading the Word. As soon as Satan sees you trying to live for the Lord, he will attack you in every area of your life. This is his job according to John 10:10a. And, he is merciless. If you are not knowledgeable about how the Word says to fight Satan, you will lose that battle and, in many cases, you could lose your life.

But, if you are empowered by the Word and the Holy Spirit, not only can you defeat Satan, but you can also save the very people you left behind in the world. Christ does not allow you to come to Him just for your own sake. He wants every one of His people to recognize who He is (1 Timothy 2:4). And, Christ will send you back from where you came to bring to Him those people you left behind. It is not enough that we are saved; Christ desires that all people be saved, and He will surely use you to help Him bring it about.

Then, in order for God to bless you, you must be positioned properly. Understand that God desires you to experience fullness of life and that the fullness is not determined by your income or background. He wants all believers to live an abundant life (John 10:10b), and He blesses us so that we have access to whatever we need to achieve this.

But, if we are disobedient, we will find ourselves out from under God's covering, which suggests that we are out of the realm of His blessing. It is as if we had been late for a gathering and discovered that all the giveaways had been dispersed at the beginning of the party. It does not mean you were not deserving of a gift or would not have received one had you been there. But, as with God's blessings, you simply were not positioned properly to receive it.

Finally, God desires that you recognize His power in your life so you can praise Him for it. We humans have the self-absorbed view that we are on earth to do whatever it is we think we should be doing. The truth is that our sole purpose for being created is to praise God. How many of us are not living according to that purpose? Why is it so difficult for even Christians to consistently give God the praise?

We would rather praise the person God moved upon to give us a job than God. We offer praise to the one who gave us a pay raise rather than to the true source of our prosperity. We emphasize the love of a man or woman rather than the love of God who transcends all earthly affections. If you are cognizant that He has ever moved on your behalf, then you have the responsibility to give God praise. Every ounce of our energy should be directed towards praising God, because ultimately that is how we come to love Him more deeply.

Our relationship with Christ allows us to release our past and embrace our present. But, how does knowing Him affect our future? Christ allows us to envision our future differently. Prior to knowing Christ, you may have imagined various things for your future that God never intended for you. But, because He was not a part of your planning process, you did not know you were moving out of His will for your life.

So, what is the variable that integrates the diverse components of the Christian life and synthesizes our past and present with our future? It is character. Our character is shaped through the process of learning who we are in Christ. It is defined by the sundry experiences, triumphs and failures we experience in attempting to rise to the expectations of Christian living. It is what gives us success when we are strong, and results in defeat when we are lacking.

It is critical that we shape our character, because it is the key to true success. Many of us leave our future behind us because of our lack of character. Our moral fiber is weak and thus does not direct us into the path God has chosen for our life. If we are not spiritually strong, then we will tend to shy away from the challenges of Christian living. And, it may have been those very challenges that God planned to use to develop our character so we would not miss what He had planned for our future. How we respond to God's call in the present is directly related to the type of future we will have. If we ignore God's call altogether, it is probable that we have abandoned the opportunity for a blessed future.

You can leave your future behind you by living in the past. Satan wants you to believe that because you made some unwise decisions, you are not worthy to move forward. There are people who are so overwhelmed by their past failures that it is difficult for them to even lift their heads up. And, the problem with not being able to forgive yourself is that you will not see God reaching down for you or who you can become. You have to release to God the dilemmas in which you find yourself and say, "Lord, I'm not just coming up, I'm coming out because I want to experience what You have in store for me."

Perfection is never attained, but you grow character by trying to reach it (Philippians 3:13-14). You can choose either success or failure. There will always be some difficult times in life, but it is the how you deal with those times that makes the difference. Do you handle your problems with an unaided reason, or do you allow God to move on your behalf? How do you engage your substance in your struggles? It is how you engage your power and ability that determines who you are and what you will achieve. You make that choice.

You choose where you want to be today and tomorrow. But, the gauge by which you measure yourself is character. Where are you compared to where you were a year ago? Are you at the same level as last year, last month, even yesterday? Have you progressed at all? You have the power to choose, but where are you? Whether you go up or down, spiral or move laterally is up to you.

While our behavior is a good indicator of our character, our thoughts offer even more persuasive evidence of who we are. This is because whatever we do occurred as a thought first and was simply manifested in the flesh. Are your thoughts as negative and worldly as they were before you came to Christ? Examine for yourself where there has been a substantial change in your life. In Mark 16:17b, the Scripture states that one of the signs of new life in Christ is that "...they shall speak with new tongues." This new tongue is the spiritual language God gives us and relates to being positive about where we are and what we are doing.

This new tongue is a heavenly language that is conducive to and reflects Christian living. There is an unknown tongue to which the Spirit of God gives utterance, but the person speaking in an unknown tongue does not understand what he is saying, so that interpretation is necessary. But, the new tongue of Mark 16:17 is the result of change in your behavior and attitude as well as the new birth. When you experience the new birth, it changes who you are. Furthermore, what you speak is now contingent upon what you possess: if you do not possess anything new, you will not speak anything new.

Your habitual pattern of thought has brought you to the place where you are today. If you are yet living in doubt and fear, your thought process is responsible for that. And, if you are moving forward, your thoughts contributed to that as well.

Your thought process dictates where you will be in life, because it is the impetus that propels you.

Nobody is responsible for your destiny in life but you. You have the responsibility to make the right choices so that you can move in the direction that is best for you. Your thoughts and behavior will determine your future. So, ask yourself: "Are you on the right course to get from where you are now to where you really want to be?"

Some of you may reflect back on your life and realize that God has used you already, and that is tremendous. But, do you not believe there is room for progress in your life and the lives of those around you? Doors have been opened for you at various points in your life, but are there not doors yet to be opened? Ways have been made, but there are still greater ways you can take to arrive at your destination in life. Is there another avenue you can travel that would bring you the kind of success you want? Not only material success, but success in regard to your mind, attitude, personality and health.

There comes a time when Christ comes into your life and indwells your spirit. As a result, you begin to take on His likeness and as 2 Corinthians 5:17b states, "...old things are passed away;

behold, all things are become new." And, this change has nothing to do with changing one's name, moving to a different city or obtaining a new job. Those changes are superficial because they do not alter the essence of who you are. No, with this change there has been a change in your spirit.

This change in your spirit adds a different dimension to your life that you were not able to experience before. We need to reach the point where we can see ourselves as someone different from who we were. Too many Christians are the same people they have always been, and are masking that sameness in church attire rather than club clothes. They think that filling their mouths with hymns rather than secular language changes their speech. It does not matter if you speak and behave the right way if there has been no real transformation in your heart, because eventually you will get tired of playing make-believe. So, how is it possible to see yourself differently? It is possible by shaping your character. Regardless of who you are and where you have been, you can still become what you want to be.

The experienced sailor weathers both the calm and the storms of the sea as he steers his course. In like manner, we must maintain control even when we come up against invasive elements that seek to hinder our passage through life. It is time to take charge of your destiny, your thoughts, your relationships, your career and your home. According to a socio gram, it is not the person who has the title who is the leader of the group. The leader of the group is the one who causes the most interaction, the one to whom the masses respond the most. Titles and positions do not make men; men make titles and positions.

Success is within you; leadership comes from within. True leaders are born of God. Wherever you fall on that socio gram, as long as you know who you are and exemplify conviction and commitment, you will be able to weather the pressures of life. People in the world are looking for real leaders as examples. They need to see someone able to weather the storms, go through the valley, climb the mountain, and willing to stand still and see the salvation of the Lord.

Life is too important for you to give over to someone else. Do not depend on someone else to meet your needs, because when they fail you, you have really failed yourself. You are the one who needs to pray, who desires a change of direction, who needs a greater anointing, more power and a great revival in your life. You must call on God yourself and tell Him, "Lord, I need You more in my life, more in my home, and more in my workplace." Tell God when the devil is wreaking havoc in your life, and He will give you the strength to tell him, "Get thee behind Me" (Matthew 16:23).

Mark 11:22 tells believers, in essence, "If you pray and believe, you can receive; you can also speak to the mountain and tell the mountain to be removed." You can do these things through Christ. He has given you the power to stand against your enemy, so you can move forward in that knowledge. We must have the right character, not a defeatist attitude and instability. In the face of our enemy's attacks, we must show that we will stand by our values and that we amount to something in Christ's sight. Half of Satan's battles are fought in that mental realm where we struggle for a sense of self, identity, and esteem. If Satan can convince you that you are not loved or worthy before God, he has already defeated you. No need to bring out his serious arsenal; you fell under a little discouragement.

Character is the one personal quality that will ensure a truly successful future. And, when character is shaped properly, people you had a problem with and things that previously separated you will no longer be in the way. In Acts 9, Jesus wanted Ananias to go restore the vision of Saul, who was known for issuing decrees and imprisoning Christians. Jesus shared that Saul was now a praying man, and that there had been a change in his character, so that now his behavior would reflect that change. That is the power of shaping character; it can make you a new person as it did Saul.

What shapes character? You are the product of your heredity, environment, physical body, conscious and unconscious mind, experience, particular position and direction in time and space. All of these contribute to the shaping of your character, including both known and unknown power. We all know when God's power is working in our lives; it is evidenced by positive changes. But, sometimes some negative power comes your way, and you do not know why or from where it is coming. This unknown power is as instrumental as known powers in helping to define your character.

That is the reason why Paul states in Romans 8:28 that all things work together for good. Not that all things are good, but they all work together for good — the known and the unknown, the good and the bad, the successes and the failures. You have the power to synthesize all these things to control your thoughts, your emotions and your destiny. If you are going to be successful and productive, you must be consistent in your behavior, so that God can use you.

Proverbs 4:23 says, "Keep thy heart with all diligence; for out of it are the issues of life." You must keep your heart and spirit with diligence, for out of them come the issues of life. How does one do this? By attending to God's Word. Sometimes, you need to turn the TV and the radio off, and invest some time in studying God's Word. And, when you have finished studying, you need to meditate on the Word. In Joshua 1:8a, God tells Joshua, "This book of the law shall not depart out of thy mouth; but thou shalt meditate therein day and night, that thou mayest observe to do according to all that is written therein...." You must turn the Word of God over and over again within your spirit.

One of the things we can think about is the fact that we can maximize our potential. This is emphasized in Ephesians 3:20: "Now unto Him that is able to do exceeding abundantly above all that we ask or think, according to the power that worketh in us...." He is able to do more than we ask or think according to His power. This power is the potential, the ability and the substance that is within us.

We cannot allow ourselves to be conformed to this world; rather we should seek to be renewed in our mind. How is my mind renewed? By allowing the logos to come into my spirit and become a part of it. After the logos becomes a part of my spirit, it becomes the rhema, the living Word inside of me. In its application to my life, it moves out of my spirit and into my intellect, where it helps me understand who I am destined to be.

Decisions accompanied by action bring about positive results. Whatever you decide to do, act upon it. The little things you do can be just as effective as bigger things in bringing about change. A great door can swing just as well from small hinges. You may experience temporary failures, but you can still have permanent success. Occasional failures do not mean that your overall efforts will end in failure.

The most effective way to turn defeat into victory is to exhibit faith and pray. Faith is the sublime motivator, and prayer is an expression of faith that accentuates the release of the driving force of one's emotions. So many times, we do everything but pray, even though whatever is inside us can come out in prayer. The greatest power known to man is the power of prayer.

This does not refer to the ritualistic prayer many of us have been praying for years, which we know verbatim. We have to learn again how to pray. Conditions in your life will help you pray, because certain experiences will bring you to a point where your need for God is pure. And, what you say is not as important as the things you are experiencing. This is because you must learn to pray about your situation, and give attention to the things that you want.

James 5:16b states, "...the effectual fervent prayer of a righteous man availeth much." When you pray to Almighty God, you will learn to recognize His voice because He will talk back to you. If you have not heard the voice of God, it is because you have not talked to Him. He is not the kind of God that focuses on how articulate you are; His concern is simply that you go to Him in prayer. God is not moved by your intellectuality, but by your spirituality. Do you know how to reach Him and let Him know your insufficiency?

He is concerned about you and your relationship with Him. And, the way those areas are strengthened is through diligence in prayer. Every once in a while, you go through difficulties because you are trying to go it alone and will not communicate. But, He is looking for someone who will call on Him. He does answer prayers, and anytime you call or Him, He is there. So, tell the devil you are tired of being low, pushed around and knocked about. Tell him you are coming out of your past and claiming your future — you are a child of God, and you will stand your ground.

Everything that God promised you, He is going to give to you through faith and prayer. He has developed and strengthened your character to the point where you can handle both Satan's hindrances and God's blessings. You are now equipped to maximize your potential despite what society says will be your outcome. So, go on and praise God until you forget about your past. Praise Him until you can disregard those things that cause perplexities in your mind. Praise Him until you can embrace the person you have become through His love. Praise Him until you receive the epiphany that He was there all the time.

Chapter Eight

Properties of Prosperity

"Wealth is gauged by accounts, material accumulation, but most importantly by spiritual abundance."

"Beloved, I wish above all things that thou mayest prosper and be in health, even as thy soul prospereth."

3 John 2

God desires that each of us experience prosperity as a result of maximizing our potential. This prosperity will manifest itself in as many ways as the lives it touches. While the term "prosperity" usually brings to mind the concept of wealth and accumulated material possessions, God encompasses more in its meaning. Prosperity can also refer to spiritual wealth, good physical health, affluence with family and friends, a rich personal life and a general sense of well-being. Christ requires that we expand our thought process to recognize all the blessings that we can receive in abundance.

The Word shows us how the concept of prosperity can be revised. In 3 John 2, John wishes Gaius, a seemingly insignificant person in the Bible, prosperity in his life: "Beloved, I wish above all things that thou mayest prosper and be in health, even as thy soul prospereth." Gaius is not an apostle or a prophet, but a simple person like many of us in the church. Yet, John mentions him to introduce us to a figure who is not as important in himself, as he is a model of the varying aspects of prosperity.

Like Gaius, you may not have risen to any height that Christian society would recognize; you may not have been appointed a pastor, bishop, or missionary. Yet, while you may not be a leader in the church, you are significant in the sight of the Lord. In like manner, Gaius is deemed significant in God's eyes. Why is he noteworthy? It is because he recognized the work of the Lord being done through someone else (Paul). He is also important because through John's words to him, we can understand that God desires our spirituality to thrive and for our endeavors to succeed.

While Gaius may not seem to have a critical role in Biblical history, he is acknowledged because of his willingness to help in the ministry. John hears about Gaius through Paul and then writes to him to share his thoughts. The value of this exchange is that John was able to expand Gaius' participation in the ministry by sharing. If we are to maximize our potential, we must take whatever it is that we have and expand upon it. And, John understood that the way to expand upon a ministry is by sharing it. In sharing, you give up what you have, and in so doing, you gain more.

How do you achieve prosperity if you paradoxically give away what you have? You must first understand which area of your life that God wishes to prosper. Then, you can anticipate how your efforts in that area will achieve the result you desire. If God's focus is for your soul to develop and prosper, He will design experiences to test you. And, the process of going through that experience is what develops your commitment and deepens your understanding till you realize you have thrived in that task.

Prosperity should be a quality of life. It is not intended to be an attribute you earn for a period of time and then become impoverished again. It is clear that God wants His children to prosper; no one can deny the fact. We are endowed with abilities that if channeled properly, can enhance the lives of others. And, it is through this service that we achieve abundance in our own lives and in our relationship with Christ.

But, we must understand that prosperity should not be an end in itself. It is less important in terms of Christian growth that we work toward attaining prosperity than that we understand the value of the process itself. It is the life that reflects commitment, dedication and action that is in line with God's Word. We must demonstrate these qualities to achieve in the areas in which God has called us to excel.

When we are impelled to live our lives for Christ, that commitment is evident in the fruits of our efforts. No one has to wonder what philosophy of life guides us. Our speech, behavior and attitude all reflect in our level of commitment to Christian living. You cannot help but feel emotionally involved in living for Christ, and thus it becomes the most important part of your life. Furthermore, when your commitment is supported and guided by God's Word, you will begin to experience prosperity.

Our commitment is inherently related to our sense of dedication. When we show that we are constant in our purpose of living for Christ, God reveals His consistency to us in the area of prosperity. When we participate more fully in prayer, He draws us closer to Him. When we try to live by Christian guidelines, He blesses our efforts. When we demonstrate our dedication to Him, He moves in our lives in a mighty way.

The action we take with respect to God is also critical in determining our level of prosperity. How much energy do we direct toward knowing Him more deeply? What is the evidence in our lives that we serve Him? How committed are we to the ministry? When we understand that church attendance alone does not qualify as action on our part, we can examine other areas in which we can mobilize ourselves.

God is concerned about the total person. Not only does He want you to prosper in terms of materialism, but He also wants you to have the prosperity of health. The value of good health is only apparent to the ill. Yet, good health is important in allowing you to maximize your potential. If you are not in good health, you will not achieve because all of your attention will be focused on the deficiency in your body.

Your health is important to your overall sense of prosperity, and requires a degree of responsibility in terms of good eating habits and the exercise of both body and mind. We exercise our minds by stretching our mental faculties to conceive of ourselves in a maximized state. Essentially, this means envisioning ourselves in ideal circumstances. God has made it clear to us what we need to do to succeed. But, we must recognize that if we are to have the perfect mindset, we must be in good physical condition so we can move, both spiritually and physically, into the place where God would have us.

We can achieve two kinds of prosperity: divine prosperity and human prosperity. The Scriptures imply that we can have divine prosperity, which is both related to and carries distinct from the prosperity that originates from within. We may prosper by our own means, but divine prosperity originates from God and that is significant. If your prosperity comes from God, there is no one who can keep you from achieving your goals. When your efforts are divinely inspired, the effects last as long as God lasts, because He is your source of strength and success.

There is permanence in divine prosperity because you can equate what you have with what God has. Jesus was very prosperous, yet his material possessions and his attire did not indicate that. He did not have a palatial house on a hill or the finest garb, but He could have because He had all the resources to get whatever He wanted. His priority was not trying to display an image but showing who He was by what He did. Whatever He wanted to eat, He ate. Whatever He needed, He had before him. Jesus exercised what He had so that people would know He had the power to obtain. Do not try to equate prosperity with the accumulation of goods. It is good for us to have what we want, but it needs to be a result of divine prosperity working in our lives.

Divine prosperity is progressive, in that, it continuously gives us a status of well-being. Psalms

1:3 supports this thought. Remember, you are planted in His Word; consequently, in whatever condition you may be, you are content. God is working in your life, and in spite of obstacles that come your way; you are not bothered because you are content in the knowledge that God's Word is true. And, because you are constantly in His Word, you can give your mind, spirit and body completely to Him.

God's prosperity is intended for every area of our lives: spiritual, material, physical and emotional. However, it is important for our sense of balance that we do not unduly emphasize any one area. This contributes to a sense of wholeness in our lives. If we concern ourselves with only one or two dimensions of our lives, we cannot be the whole people God planned for us to be.

The prosperity that radiates from within is also a positive (albeit limited) quality. Making an effort to gain abundance in varying facets of our lives creates it. If it is physical prosperity we seek, we place our focus on exercise and nutritious eating. It is a lifestyle to which we are committed. It is something that we ourselves work toward; no one gives it to us.

The limitation of prosperity that comes from within is that it is maintained only as long as we work for it. Also, not every effort on our part is assurance of success. Unlike with divine prosperity, which has no end to its power, you must generate the rewards. While the results of the two types of prosperity could be the same, the processes of the two are different. And, it is better to be blessed with divine prosperity, because God never fails in maximizing your potential for good.

What is potential? It is substance, power and ability. How do we maximize that potential? We expand upon and increase our participation in propelling our gifts and abilities onto a greater platform that the world can benefit from. We take the substance within us, great or small, and maximize it. We capitalize on our power and ability. The greatest effect of making the most of our potential is that God is glorified through our efforts. We do not allow anyone or anything to interfere with this process. We maximize our potential because we desire to do it; we have equipped ourselves, and we are now ready to move forth.

Scripture offers support that God intended for us to prosper from the beginning. As soon as He created man, He blessed them (Genesis 1:27-28). It is God's desire that you are blessed. The moment you come to Christ and give Him your heart, you immediately come under His protection and blessing. And, by God's blessing, we can experience newness of life, so that our lives reflect those spiritual changes that occur as a result of His blessings.

When we experience new birth, we have new life. We become different creatures with a quickened spirit when we come to Christ. It does not make any difference what we were before if we allow His blessing to reform us. Adam was nothing but dust before He experienced God's blessings. He was a non-entity until God took him and formed him into something.

In like manner, it does not matter that our lives did not reflect the ideals of Christian living before we came to Christ. We do not need to regale others with the tales of our failures, our backsliding or our unfaithfulness to God. He is already aware of our deficiencies and seeks only to conform us to the image of His Son. If the past is recounted as a testimony and a means to help gauge our progress, then it has a place. But, we must be careful that highlighting our past distance from Christ does not have the effect of discouraging us from pursuing our goal of having a closer relationship with Him. For some people, seeing the entire journey from their status in life to their desired goal of unity with Christ can be simply overwhelming. It is better that we focus on where we are at this moment and how we can enhance our relationship with Christ today.

The most redeeming aspect of knowing Christ is that I have new life in Him. And, I need to recognize that new life is directly connected to prosperity. I die in regard to the influence of the flesh on my spirit and mind. And, I say to God, "Lord, I surrender who I am so that I may become the real person that You want me to be." When I die to self and have new life in Christ, I am blessed.

The process of new birth requires the reception of God's Spirit to be blessed. Why are we blessed? We need only consider the experience of Adam to understand the source of our blessings. When Adam was made in God's image, he partook of all of the characteristics that God had. God was creative in His design of the world. He was progressive in that He created resources for life throughout the ages. God had a positive attitude, a sense of direction, knowledge, wisdom, purpose and meaning. Since God exemplified these characteristics and others, so it was with Adam. In the same way, we take on these qualities of God through the new birth.

What happens when you experience the new birth? A quickened spirit and the attributes of God are yours as a result. Then, you are able to apply those qualities in your own life as God has within His. Is that not powerful? When you come to Christ, you are given access to the attributes of God. And, like Gaius, no matter how insignificant you may feel or how unimportant you may be in the eyes of others, you can change things in your life because God has given you the power to do it.

An idea that many Christians relate to new birth is God's command to be fruitful and multiply. Yet, this is a concept that must be revisited to comprehend the totality of meaning that God intended. Many people believe that God was referencing only to having children. If that were true, then many of us would be living in disobedience since married people have figured out how not to have children. So, we must understand that from the beginning, God wanted you to be fruitful. And, yes, He wanted man to continue to populate the land. But, it is critical that you also understand that God intended for you to be fruitful in every area of your life.

God wants you to expand your talents and abilities in every area of your life. Maximize your substance until you are financially secure, experiencing job satisfaction, having deepened your relationships with friends and family — in short, until you feel whole again. Multiply not only biologically, but also in terms of prayer, charity, ministry and love. Do not be content with the status quo. When you have maximized your potential in all areas of your life, you will be able to take control of your environment with the power that you have acquired.

How do we know that we are able to take control of situations in our lives? We know from the Word that God has given us dominion over everything that moves. Consequently, He expects us to deal with things in the manner in which they should be dealt. We must understand that as God is sovereign in the universe, Also, He has made man sovereign on earth. We have been delegated responsibility over powers both seen and unseen.

Yet, we allow everything to control us, rather than controlling everything ourselves. Man has been given power, authority and ability to rule over everything. That includes dominating the situations in our lives. If you accept that God has delegated a certain responsibility to you, then what Suzy Q says about you should not throw you off balance. When men do not choose you to be a part of their inner circles, you do not need to question yourself. Your sense of esteem should not rest on man's perception of you, but on your image as reflected in God.

God has given you power over your life since the beginning. It has been reinforced and enhanced upon your receiving the Holy Spirit. And, when you have that spiritual dynamo on the inside of you, there ought not be anything that can keep you from succeeding. And, how do we maintain this ruler ship in our lives? How do we maintain control over the people and forces that seek to hinder our progress? The answer is to live in obedience to the Word of God.

Whatever God tells you to do in His Word, you need to do it. We get into trouble when we try to alter a clear command from God on how to live. We try to assess His command from our intellect and say, "Surely, He wouldn't demand that level of commitment from me. Oh, that's not really what God meant in this day and time." God's Word is not negotiable, and the best assurance of our success is to line up our lives with the Word.

You have to recognize that your prosperity lies in the area to which God has called you. He has given you the ability to learn and then apply that knowledge to life. But, that application must occur where He directs; otherwise, you are applying medicine meant for a different symptom and there is no sense of wholeness. God has equipped you to do a certain thing, and He wants you to maximize your potential accordingly. And, since not everyone has been called in the same area (1 Corinthian 7:7), you must be sensitive to God's voice so you will utilize your potential properly.

The power that we have to reign in life will only continue as long as we are faithful and obedient to God and His Word. If you are doing these things, then you ought to be able to maximize your potential and gain a greater portion from the little that you currently have. Luke 11:9 says, "Ask, and it shall be given you; seek, and ye shall find; knock, and it shall be opened unto you." With the potential that you have, you need to start asking God to direct you and multiply your opportunities. Not only should you ask Him for things, but you must also seek His direction, so that your gifts are channeled correctly. "What is Your will for my life? What do You desire that I do? Where should I go?" If the essential aspects of Christian living are not presented to God, then, for whom are you truly living? So, asking of God and understanding His response defines the primary stage of Christian growth.

When we have received God's response, it should lead us to seek understanding on that issue. It serves no purpose for someone to give us instructions if we do not know how to follow them. So many times we are required to seek further in God's Word, so we will know how to greater maximize what we have. More importantly, we must seek Him, so that we will know Him better and deepen our relationship with Christ.

Then, we must enter the "knocking" stage in our Christian growth, because this is an indicator to God of our sincerity. The fact that you have been obedient in your discipline, righteous in your lifestyle, and consistent in your behavior allows you to enter into a place where God can move through you. Your spiritual condition causes you to knock, because you know you are recognized by heaven. It is rare that a person seeks entrance into a place where they do not believe they would be welcomed.

It is what you have within you that bombards heaven and responds to your knocks. That substance within is what splits asunder the elements that come against you, and makes what is chaotic in your life come together and form a sense of purpose and direction.

You cannot maximize your potential if you are spreading your talents into an abundance of areas. "A double-minded man is unstable in all his ways" (James 1:8). If you do not know what to do, the Holy Spirit can give you a sense of direction, and then you must follow that route. Know what you want to be early and set your course. When you gain focus on what it is that you want to do, persistent focus allows you to receive what you want. Your potential is greater than what others see. You know for yourself who you are and where you ought to be. Others do not know what you need or who you are. It is so important that you recognize this truth, because too many people look to others to show them where they should be in life. And, the reality is that only God is aware of the depth of your potential.

John 15:1 says, "I am the True Vine, and My Father is the Husbandman." If Christ is the True Vine and you are in Him, and there is no question in terms of His identity, then there should be no question about of who you are. You are connected to the source of your spiritual growth. Christ has already identified himself as your source of the Word, and says that you need only remain a part of Him to continue to grow. John 15:7 confirms this, "If ye abide in Me, and My words abide in you, ye shall ask what ye will, and it shall be done unto you."

The finest of grapes come from the vine that has been nurtured in the proper type of soil. The soil determines what type of grapes will be produced. So, if your source of power is Christ, you are assured of producing great things. But, if you depend on earthly substance, you will never fully develop in the manner that Christ desires for you. The fruit of the vine has nothing to do with its growth; the vine is the life support system. It is the vine that has resources coming into it. It is the vine that takes water and nutrients from the ground to nourish the fruit. All of the components necessary for the growth of the fruit must come through the vine.

And, it is the vinedresser who is responsible for seeing that the vine is intact and prepared and properly dressed so that growth will come to the fruit. The fruit has only to get there. In John 15:16, Jesus says, "Ye have not chosen Me, but I have chosen you, and ordained you, that ye should go and bring forth fruit, and that your fruit should remain: that whatsoever ye shall ask of the Father in My Name, He may give it you." Jesus is telling us that if we are in Him and desire something, we are going to receive it because the Father is concerned about Him and is going to make sure His friends have provisions. Jesus is essentially asking us to understand that His Father cannot take care of Him and neglect us at the same time, since we are in Him. In like manner, why should a fetus worry about food? When the mother eats, the fetus eats. How can a pregnant woman satisfy her own appetite without satisfying that of the baby within her?

Our ability and potential to prosper is heightened when we serve others. We have to give of ourselves to others for God to bless and enhance what we have. Luke 12:15 says, "Take heed, and beware of covetousness: for a man's life consisteth not in the abundance of the things which he possesseth." As you maximize your potential, you will experience an increase. But, the increase is given so that we may share with others. Whatever you have given up is not greater than the Father, who will replenish your gift a hundred fold. As you share the anointing and the blessings in your life, your potential becomes that much greater.

Every time you pay tithes, give an offering and assist others, you are maximizing your potential. This is because you are laying up treasure in heaven, and God's return is beyond your comprehension. And, He gives a return to us when we serve His people. When you help others, God recognizes that spirit in you and gives you more energy, resources and power and a greater anointing.

Ephesians 3:20 states, "Now unto Him that is able to do exceeding abundantly above all that we ask or think, according to the power that worketh in us...." The Word is essentially saying that you have just as much as Christ has, and the reason is that He is at work within you. His power is within you. Your friends and your bank account do not limit God. He does not offer you a pre-approved blessing and then withdraw it when all your history is exposed. What God has for you cannot be contained because it permeates the very essence of your spirit.

Psalms 24:1 tells us, "The earth is the Lord's, and the fullness thereof." You cannot limit God. You cannot limit what He has for you in terms of potential. And, your ability to maximize is greater than what you can ask; it has not even entered your imagination. You cannot conjure up the things God will allow you to do in terms of work and creative processes. You can do far more than what you imagine. The power of God works in you. You must utilize your potential to make your prosperity a reality.

In the final analysis, none of our accumulated wealth can save our souls. Christ does not receive us into His bosom based on our assets. While being healthy is a state for which we should strive, it does not gain an advantage for us with Christ. It is fulfilling to have an abundance of people who surround you with their warmth and love, yet you must still stand alone before God. Yet, Christ promises us the greater possibility of spiritual prosperity, because we can leave it behind to bless others' lives and have it catapult us into heaven. It is the only facet of prosperity that serves as both loner and companion to our soul.